Coaching
Beyond The Lines

Influence, Inspiration, Integrity, and Impact

DeAngelo Wiser

Oakamoor Publishing

Published in 2025 by Oakamoor Publishing, an imprint of Bennion Kearny Limited.

ISBN: 978-1-910773-89-5

Published by Oakamoor Publishing, Bennion Kearny Limited
6 Woodside
Churnet View Road
Oakamoor
Staffordshire
ST10 3AE

www.BennionKearny.com

DEDICATION

Western Kentucky University Women's Soccer Coach, Jason Neidell has been a huge mentor for me throughout my career. It all started when my teams first attended his team camps, followed by his willingness to give me a role in his camp staff, allowing me to put together videos, conduct team-building activities with all the teams, and all the while trusting and seeing more in me than I saw in myself. His players are so blessed to have him. His focus has always and continues to be on others first.

A beautiful game brought us together, our shared drive to humbly influence others was our bond, but his unselfish willingness to believe in me will always be a reminder of our ability to positively influence players, coaches, parents, and others who depend on us.

While others were skeptical and asked, "What could I possibly do?" He said, "Come on down."

Thank you doesn't come close to how much he impacted my life. I will forever be grateful.

Table of Contents

FOREWORD

As a former college coach and now a developer of people, I have come to appreciate the profound impact a dedicated mentor can have on those they lead. Coach DeAngelo Wiser epitomizes this influence, demonstrating a commitment to investing in people that is both rare and invaluable in today's world.

Throughout his career, DeAngelo has embodied the core principles of influence, impact, inspiration, and integrity, not just in his coaching but in every facet of his life. His dedication goes beyond developing his players' athletic abilities; he is passionately committed to nurturing the personal growth and development of every individual who crosses his path.

One of DeAngelo's gifts is his willingness to share what he has learned with others. In a world where many guard their knowledge and ideas out of fear that others might surpass them, DeAngelo stands out. He genuinely wants others to succeed and is generous in imparting his wisdom and experiences. This selflessness is a testament to his character and his belief in the power of collective growth and improvement.

In this book, DeAngelo shares his insights, offering readers a treasure trove of valuable lessons that extend far beyond the playing field. His words are not merely advice; they are a reflection of a life lived with purpose and dedication to uplifting others.

I have no doubt that you, the reader, will find immense value in DeAngelo's teachings. His experiences and reflections will ignite thoughts, ideas, and motivations that you can carry with you, not only in your career but in your journey as a mentor and leader.

May this book inspire you to continue being the role model and voice of reason your players and peers need. As DeAngelo has shown us, it is through our unwavering commitment to others that we leave a lasting legacy.

Molly Grisham

INTRODUCTION

We've always been told, "The game is a great teacher." Within the lines of the pitch, so many moments, situations, and challenges test our players' ability to succeed. During those moments, our players grow, learn, and work through building confidence.

But what about the situations players face away from the field or school, where coaches aren't present? Those moments *beyond the lines*. Those moments they're tempted to do something they know is wrong. On game day, players have the support of teammates and coaches. After a game, a day off, or in the classroom, how will they handle real-life issues such as failing a class, personal issues with teammates, or running with classmates who have no respect for accountability?

Do your players embrace the expectations set by you and the team? Do they carry them to *every* place or situation they work through? Have you made your message clear? Although tactics, strategy, skill, fitness, and competition are hallmarks that define our players, it is personal responsibility away from the field that requires their greatest personal discipline.

Four things – influence, impact, inspiration, and integrity – are the pillars of our leadership philosophy. We will cover them all over the following pages.

My hope is that you find something in this book that ignites a thought, an idea, a motivation that you can carry to your team during difficult times and utilize throughout your career. I wish you and your team the best. Keep inspiring your players and being the role model and voice of reason they need to see and hear.

INFLUENCE

ATTITUDES: WHERE WILL YOU DRAW THE LINE?

Have you encountered a player or players who – over the course of a season – you simply couldn't reach? They always seemed to look at you skeptically with "locked out" body language when you addressed the team, and never appeared to trust you or anyone else. Where did that come from? *Why should they change? Will their attitude be detrimental to the team?*

We all understand that attitudes are shaped and based on life experiences, either through our family or situations with others. Often, those experiences aren't very pleasant, and thus, a mistrustful attitude is born. Plus, many parents teach their children to be skeptical of everyone they meet as a safeguard. I think you'd agree that's a good approach today in a lot of settings. The question is, should it last a lifetime with everyone our player meets, and can it be changed or altered if necessary?

Should we be obsessed with changing the attitudes of our players to our way of thinking? I think not. Give thought to your personality and level of trust. Can it be a benefit to have players with the opposite perspective? Without a doubt! Just by disagreeing, they often cause us to rethink the activity, strategy, and ways to get through to our players. The key is teaching our players not to change their attitudes necessarily, but to deal with situations in a respectful and "Let's See" manner.

What is a "Let's See" manner? Players *wait* to see how something plays out, the benefit it may have for them, and whether it might just be a good thing. All we're doing is asking them to change the lens they look through and be a little more flexible. Every time they are, it builds trust and – over the course of time – shifts the outlook from, "I hate doing this" to "Wow! This isn't bad" and "I had no idea this would help me and the team so much."

Attitudes, unlike skills, can take a long time to adjust, and very often you may never see any change. That doesn't mean you stop trying, though. Change takes a lot of patience and, at times, tolerance to work through the lessons of an understanding and accepting attitude. So, how can you get started?

1. Meet with the player(s). Let them know you sense some skepticism. Ask for their feedback and see if they will share where it originates.
2. Let them know what kind of coach you are, and what you expect from every player.
3. Ask how attitudes and outlooks might impact a player and the team.
4. Share your ideas on how players should address areas they don't agree with. Ask for their thoughts.
5. Explain that your door is always open should they want to discuss anything.
6. Do your best never to call out this player harshly, or any player, in front of the team. It could destroy any good work accomplished.
7. Avoid giving this player any special treatment because you feel especially bad about past experiences in their life.
8. Be consistent with your words and actions. All players must be held accountable in practice/games and for conduct at school and in the community.
9. Remember to call on them, as well as other players, from time to time with thoughts about what they accomplished in practice to end the day.
10. Pair them up or put them in a strong group that can help with any issues they may be having.

We often shy away from allowing this player or players an opportunity to speak in front of the team, unsure of what they might say. How about calling on them and showing how proud we are of the road they've traveled and where they're headed?

You may want to put them in a leadership role (as well as other players) for a day to see what it's like. They may gain an appreciation for what you do and see firsthand that it's not easy taking care of so many players and viewpoints.

Another reason behind a player's skeptical attitude may be boredom. They may not see the justification or reasoning for many repetitions of a particular skill or play. Explaining the "why" and how it will help them and the team may be all they need.

Just because they're skeptical in the beginning doesn't mean they need to be like this across their whole career. Keep working to break down that barrier; it will be worth it.

DIVISIVENESS: IS IT YOU?

Are you battling or creating animosity and division within your team? I know you would never do it on purpose because you want to bring your team together for one vision, one mission and one reward.

But think about your own family. Was there a favorite sister or brother who appeared to get more love and attention than you? Was it just your perception, or was it really that way? Is it the same today? Do your parents even realize what they're doing? Did you ever approach them concerning your apparent slight? Did it upset you?

Is that situation possible with your players? Do they perceive you show favoritism toward a certain player or players time after time? Have you ever been approached by other players about it? You might say, "Well, I do have favorites." It's the players who give maximum effort in practice and games, who act responsibly, help their teammates, and have a wonderful attitude. I feel certain most of us would agree with all those positive attributes. But is that where the animosity grows?

So, what is the lightning rod that rips at the very fiber of building a cohesive team where players are asked – by you – to give up themselves and everything selfish for their teammates to accomplish great things? It's often the recognition we, as coaches, offer. This includes the things we say verbally, how we act in front of the team, and the awards we hand out at the end-of-year banquet (typically displayed on social media for all to see).

Let's think back to what we just said. We're asking every player to give up themselves as individuals for the benefit of the team, and then after practice, after a game, or the end-of-year banquet, we highlight or go overboard with our words about individual players. Can you see and hear the struggle they're having with this? What can you do? Where can you turn?

Let's visit one end-of-season award that seems to cause the most anger, the MVP. Now, I bet if you asked every player individually who the best player on your team is, they would almost unanimously agree on one individual, and it would be the one you would also choose. So, what's the issue? The issue is how you celebrate this player in front of an audience of parents, coaches, media, and your team. Will you go on and on about this player more than any other player on your team? Will you hold them higher than anyone else on the team? That's the rub. They become that favorite sister or brother. Very often, we don't realize how over the top we go on about this player because we're so glad they're on our team and what they can do!

I will say these issues can become bigger with an immature team, a team that is a group of selfish individuals, or a great player who flaunts his or her talents in the faces of their less skilled teammates. You'll see these flaws throughout the year in other situations as you do your best to shape the culture of your team.

I believe you can prepare your players by explaining – before the season begins – what you're looking for in practice and games, the awards that will be handed out, the criteria to be considered, those who will decide, and your philosophy on what it all means. It won't soften the blow to a player who feels they should have won a certain award, but they were informed and can approach you if they need to voice their opinion.

I handed out an MVP award in my first year of coaching. There was no doubt who that player was. My players knew it as well. Didn't matter. As we prepared for a game the following season, I asked my leaders to take care of an important task. One of them looked at me and said, "Why don't you ask Renee? She's your MVP." The message was clear, and from that day forward, I never handed out another MVP award. You could say that by doing so, I let them win, but when I saw the divisiveness it created, it wasn't worth destroying our team.

I also had an incident at an in-season tournament where we lost both games and played terribly. As we were walking toward the bus, the tournament director stopped me and said, "Coach, your team gets one all-tournament selection. Who will it be?" as he handed me the award. I handed it back to him and said, "Give it to a team more deserving," as I walked away.

You have to decide how important individual awards are within a team game. Awards such as All-American, All-State, and All-Conference that are voted on by others are great and much earned. Others from you – such as Defensive and Offensive Player of the Year – are easily compiled based on statistics and justified. It's just those awards such as Most Improved or MVP that might be seen as a favorite sister or brother award. You might think a while on whether they're worth it or not.

ENGAGEMENT IN YOUR MEETINGS

How would you rate your team meetings? Not the ones where you hand out uniforms and awards or go to a nice restaurant. I'm talking about task-oriented meetings such as game plans, video reviews, expectations, and information sharing. Are you ever frustrated, or do you feel they're just a task you must complete? After all, there are many responsibilities to take care of on any given day, and then to have a meeting later that day can feel like drudgery. What about the players? Are they usually happy to be there, or is it a grind for them too?

Think about this question, "Do you put as much work into planning and organizing those meetings as you do with practice?" Only you can answer that, but it is worth considering. I know most coaches are meticulous in planning every detail of practice, knowing it may mean the difference in their next game. Is that true of your meetings?

How can you enliven meetings and reach your players? In a time of increasing technology and advances, every new device or phone pulls your players in a different direction with sparkling images, faraway places, texts, sounds, and music. How can you possibly compete with that?

The days of a coach standing in front of the team and talking continuously are over. Oh, sure, you can do it for a few minutes, but try doing it for 10 or 15 minutes and look around. You'll see heads down or blank stares. You lost them after that first minute or two. Players are more visually inclined than ever before. Plus, they're conditioned to answer every text immediately, regardless of where they are or what they're doing!

Some coaches might say if players aren't paying attention, they'll be held accountable in practice or ultimately pay the price when questioned about what the instructions were. However, should we be fighting technology or finding new ways to use it to enhance our meetings?

Let's consider some guidelines and suggestions for making our meetings more successful:

1. Assign work (that will be used) *before* the meeting.
2. Consider separate groups if a particular subject doesn't pertain to everyone, such as defenders and goalkeepers only, or strikers and midfielders.
3. Engage all learning styles as much as possible with visual and auditory aides, as well as kinesthetic activities.
4. You're the star; give your best performance. Remember, you're not there to hand out papers.
5. Begin the presentation with a powerful or entertaining video clip.
6. Follow with the statement of, "We are here tonight to…"
7. Keep the meeting on task. If other subjects are brought up to discuss, agree on another place and time to examine them, such as "the practice field".
8. Consider limiting players to 45 seconds for answers so the meeting keeps moving and stays on track.

As you know, the lead-in video clip is a big key to grab a player's attention. It could relate to the meeting topic or just be a funny or hilarious clip, which you – at some point – tie into the topic later on. I would also recommend some video or music along the way if the presentation is more than 15 or 20 minutes. If technology is not your expertise, get someone in the technology department, a student, or even a player to assist you.

We also need to consider whether the meeting is necessary. Or, at least, could part of it be accomplished (voting, selecting, developing a list, etc.) before players arrive? If it's necessary, remember players' attention spans are short. Keep it lively, engaging, and entertaining. Certainly, getting players up and moving, or putting them in groups with an icebreaker activity are options (as well as team-building activities and/or group tasks).

Let's look at some key points to consider:

1. Respect players' time; keep the meeting short and on point. Finish on time.
2. Divide the players up differently for every meeting, and give every player the opportunity to be a group leader at some point in the year.

3. When you speak, get to the point – the "why" we are here.
4. Engage players/ask questions, such as "How does this relate to us?" And listen!
5. End with clear directions and tasks. Remember, the meeting isn't the end; it's just the beginning.
6. Ask the players if they have anything else to add or whether they have any questions.
7. Thank them for their attention and participation.

Could there be a way to share the meeting's responsibilities with your players? Let's look at conducting a meeting into game footage or an opponent, and ways we can engage our players.

1. Share certain clips with the players online or through apps. Do your best to avoid saying, "Watch the first half, or watch the whole game." Pick out *specific* moments.
2. Make it a player's responsibility to view it.
3. During (or after) viewing, have the players list three areas we could use to exploit the other team, or where we could have improved in our previous game.
4. Place players in small groups to discuss and present their findings at the meeting. Teach players to question each other using "why" or "how".
5. The group leader introduces one area noted by each player in their group to discuss, then presents it to the whole team.
6. Record findings on the board and let the whole team discuss, agree, and/or disagree while setting priorities.
7. At each meeting, form different groups that connect on the field, such as strikers/midfielders, midfielders/defenders, defenders/goalkeeper.
8. If you want to make the meeting more personal, you could bring snacks and drinks. Offering a comfortable setting sets a positive tone.
9. One of the key elements is how you end any meeting and your team's work. It must be important to you and the success of the team, and they need to hear you say that. It simply has to be more than a task.

10. Competing with or becoming a technology wizard isn't something to shy away from. There will always be distractions for your players as they grow. Think back to the distractions you faced as a player. Yes, they've changed and seem more pronounced than ever before, but your willingness to care about your players, listen to their ideas, and embrace their youthful enthusiasm is what really matters. Just keep them engaged and adjust accordingly.

Regardless of the subject of team meetings, they allow your players to buy into ownership of the team, how they can work together in every challenge, and what they have to do to improve for success. It's a daunting task to build a house single-handedly, but if everyone on your team grabs a hammer and nails – allowing them to put their special touches on it – it becomes much more than a house. It becomes a home, and isn't that a better description of *where* you want your team to be?

Begin today to set meeting priorities for your season and plan them out with the same attention to detail as your practices. It will make a difference.

MOTIVATION OR MAGIC?

What motivates *you*? Does it play a part in how you motivate your team? Does it impact your ability to motivate your team effectively? I believe it does. There are certain topics, activities, and concepts we feel comfortable with, allowing us to convey our message sincerely, while other motivation techniques may not feel quite right.

We've all searched for that magic formula to propel our team to success. Does it exist? Contrary to conventional wisdom, I believe it does. The secret is realizing it exists in *many* forms and shapes for *different* teams and *different* circumstances.

Have you tried to motivate your team, but it failed miserably? How did you know? Was it because you lost the game? Maybe it worked, and the score wouldn't have been as close if you had used nothing. Did you ever think a lesson more important than a win might be learned? Motivation is hard to measure, and our measurements are often wins and losses.

A Moment of Motivation I'll never forget...

This was the big night. Tension was everywhere. We had advanced to the state tournament, and a trip to the final four was on the line. The day before, I had stayed at the field after practice and spent a couple of hours sitting on our bench, thinking of the best way to motivate our team.

I played the game in my mind as I sat there and wondered what it would take to give our team the edge. Too much motivation would make us nervous early in the game and might work against us; too little, and we'd be flat and vulnerable to giving up a goal.

Finally, after arriving home feeling overwhelmed with too many ideas to think about, my phone rang. It was Janie, who had played on one of our previous regional championships teams but had moved away. She wanted to wish us the best of luck and was sorry she couldn't be there to cheer us on. You could sense the sincerity in her voice.

After telling her we'd have our hands full and the challenges we faced, she came up with an idea that was truly wonderful. She reminded me of a tradition we had of giving jerseys to former players after a few years if they wanted them, and said she wanted me to cut her's up and give a piece to each player to put in their sock for the game.

If she couldn't be there, she wanted a former champion's spirit riding with each player during the game. "Wow!" was all I could say. I had no problem relaying her message in a heartfelt way to our team before the game. As I cut the jersey in front of our players and handed it out, I could see by their expressions that motivation need not be loud and theatrical. The connection to another champion – and her willingness to sacrifice for players she didn't know – was felt by everyone. Nothing else had to be said.

On that night, we were defeated by a better team, but the motivation given to us by Janie would allow us to play the best game of the year. Clearly, the lesson learned from her willingness to give was more important than the game.

I believe several ingredients must be in place for motivation to be effective.

Let's mention seven:

1. **Real/Sincere.** Is it real and sincere? Players know when your efforts are sincere. Do you really believe in your message and what you're asking the players to do? Is it just some theatrical performance or a gimmick to get the team pumped up? Theatrics or trashing the other team before the game usually only last for a couple of minutes, and then the higher-skilled team takes over.

2. **From each other.** Players need to hear what this game or post-season means from each other. For seniors, it's their last chance; for others, it may be the sacrifice they've made to be on the team, or a loved one struggling with life. It may simply be what their teammates mean to them. Get them started and then fade into the background, listening in awe at your players' dedication and heartfelt messages.

3. **Audience.** When you motivate your team, are you reaching them all? Probably not, but are you reaching the key players? Every player is motivated in different ways, so make sure your leaders understand your message. Their ability to convey that message in words and actions to the rest of the team will make the difference.

4. **Benefits.** What's in it for the team? It can't be just for you. Do they really want to achieve the championship or win on this night? Remind them of all they've done to prepare for this game. They play the game, so build the value for them.

5. **Credible.** Motivation can be overdone. If you've torn the other team's jersey and ripped up press clippings before every game, your act is probably getting old with the team. Save the true motivation for key games when the team understands you really mean it, and it's not another act.

6. **Threatening or rewarding.** Negative motivation can work against the team. Placing them in a mental state of fear of losing the contest and how it can impact the team rarely works out. A scared team usually plays scared. Use your motivation to explain the rewards that come with playing a great game.

7. **Worth it.** Paint a picture for your team when motivating them. Some have never been where you believe your team is capable of going. It has to be worth the commitment for your motivation to work. A former or current player speaking before the game can paint the picture you need.

Rah-Rah motivation before a game usually only lasts for a few minutes, and then skill level, determination, and preparation take over. Don't spend too much time on some far-out motivation technique or theatrics to pump your team up. Great teams know what they need to do to be successful.

Here are some reminders for your team heading to the post-season:

1. The sacrifice and commitment they've put in to get here.
2. How proud you are of their efforts and how proud you are to be their coach.
3. Highlight their accomplishments to this point.
4. Who they represent.
5. What they are capable of.

6. How much they mean to each other.
7. Moments like this are once in a lifetime.
8. How much confidence you have in them.
9. Those who have worn the jersey they have on tonight.
10. Never be satisfied with where you are, only where you're going.

The best time to motivate your team is during and after practice every day. By doing so, it becomes a habit and part of who they are, not just for the big game, but for every challenge they face in life. Remind your players of the goals the team sets for the season the individual goals they set for themselves, and the importance it carries when the post-season begins. By doing so, you remind them of the motivation necessary to be successful.

As far as that last-minute speech to your team, I would say to keep it brief and to the point. There's no magic for your team tonight, just heartfelt and confident words.

No one says it better than Hall of Fame Swimming Coach Dave Barney as he gives his swimmer last-second instructions and wisdom before her final race. "Nothing I can say to you now will be of much use to you in that last 15 or so yards to the finish. You're on your own, so to speak. And, for what it's worth, I want you to know that I'd much rather it be in your hands and in your heart than in mine. You're a champion . . . a thoroughbred . . . finish like one."

POSSIBLE, WHAT'S ON THE OTHER SIDE?

What's possible in your career as a player or coach?

Possible is such an intriguing word. So many thoughts come to mind as you say it. You see yourself making dreams come true, such as winning championships, scoring the winning goal, making that defensive play to win the game, and so much more. Possible makes us think about – and create – a vision of what we could become or accomplish.

Remember those times when you were dared to ride a rollercoaster, cliff dive, rappel, zipline, dive off the high board at the pool, or try out for a sports team? Possible was etched in your mind with thoughts of, 'Can I do this?'. Remember the feeling of accomplishment after you showed others – and more importantly, you proved to yourself – that you had what it takes to look a challenge in the eye and win.

So, what causes that dream or vision to disappear or fade away?

A lack of commitment and determination are the biggest deterrents. Daydreaming is easy, seeing ourselves in that spotlight, but then we return to reality and see that river, canyon, or mountain that we'd have to cross or climb to accomplish so many great things.

If you climb Long's Peak in Colorado, you'll have to hike and then climb; no ski lifts to take you to the top. If you want to really experience the Grand Canyon, you'll hike to the bottom with a pack and then do it in reverse to get back out. For many, that mountain is too high and the canyon too deep, but 'staying where you are' is like rollercoasters and ziplines – they're easy and spoil us. You just hook on, climb, or ride.

When we see that canyon or mountaintop top, we begin to wonder how in the world we can get there. Should we even try? Is it worth all the time and effort we'll have to endure? What about everything we may have to give up?

Let's face it, the easiest plan is to stay where you are; after all, it's not that bad. Nothing wrong with being a middle-of-the-road coach or player, and still having time for all your friends plus the free time to do anything you want.

But if you're a competitor, that word "possible" keeps drawing you in. You see others who went on that journey discover who they were and what they could become. Have you ever thought what it would be like to be on the other side of possible?

We all know a few colleagues or friends who were transformed as they dedicated themselves to turning possible into a reality.

Make no mistake, it's not the river, canyon, or mountain that turns so many away. They will always be there. It's the individual taking the easy, comfortable path in their life or career. Are there any drawbacks to staying in that comfortable place in your career? Let's look at some considerations:

1. Will you look back with disappointment later in life because you didn't take that challenge to see what you could accomplish?
2. Have you considered how crossing that river or canyon, or climbing that mountain, doesn't mean you have to be someone else when it's over?
3. You may only get one chance in your career to go on this journey. Will you recognize that?
4. How will you ever know what you could have accomplished without challenging yourself to see what is possible?
5. Where you are now will always be there, but do you long for more?
6. Should you only get halfway across on your attempt, you will have gone farther than most. And you will know more about yourself than ever before.

What language do you use with your players? Are you constantly challenging them to cross that river or canyon, or climb that mountain to become a better player or version of themselves? Do you know what that involves? How can you inspire them to yearn to see what's on the other side of possible if *you* are reluctant?

"If you want to build a ship, don't drum up people to collect wood and don't assign them tasks and work, but rather teach them to long for the endless immensity of the sea." Antoine de Saint-Exupery

This quote may help to inspire your players. You can build that longing for the sea through your vision, your interpretation, or your experience and words describing the river, the canyon, or the mountain as a magnificent challenge to be conquered. In our case, it is what's on the other side of "possible" for them. Will they be convinced?

What about your career? Where are *you* now? Is it where you want to be in five or ten years? It is certainly fine if it is, but are there other challenges you'd like to accomplish that you feel just aren't possible at this time? Will the time ever be just right? Doubtful. If you long to coach at a higher level, become an administrator, or embrace any other job or vocation you've considered, the time may be now.

That river, canyon, and mountain will always be there. It may just be time to see what's on the other side of possible. I can tell you I've seen what was on the other side of possible for me. No, I didn't accomplish great things or become an acclaimed teacher, climber, coach, author, or speaker, but I wouldn't have experienced any of the five without making it to the other side.

Start today and prove to yourself you can do it. Then go out and inspire others to do the same.

WHAT HUNGER DRIVES YOUR PLAYERS?

Look at any sportsperson who holds established records that seem unbreakable… and what do you see? Many are physical specimens with speed and power, while others are simply relentless, like distance runners stalking their opponents until the time is right to win the event.

What makes these athletes different? Are they just lucky to be born in a seemingly weak year of competition, or are they that much better? Some look like any of us in stature and could walk around a shopping mall without recognition. How were they able to accomplish something so significant?

What about coaches who hold records for championships and games won within their sport? How can they consistently beat their competition night in and night out? What makes them so special? Is it their knowledge of the game and superior intellect, longevity in their sport, an ability to motivate their players, or are they just at the right school at the right time?

We must dig a little deeper to separate these special players and coaches from their contemporaries. Something or someone along their journey became glaringly apparent, motivating them to be better than anyone else. It's called HUNGER!

When we think of being hungry, we tend to think in terms of "it's time to eat." It doesn't mean we haven't eaten in two or three days; it just means we're hungry. There's a world of difference between hungry and hunger.

As we think about definitions for hunger, we find it's a feeling of discomfort or weakness caused by a lack of food, alongside a strong desire or craving. It's easy to see the correlation when we draw a line connecting the need to accomplish great things to our definitions of hunger. Our athletes' and coaches' food, in this case, are accomplishments, and they simply won't be satisfied until they reach them.

Where does this hunger originate? I believe it comes from many sources whose mission is to motivate; sources such as parents, teachers, life experiences and – yes – players and coaches themselves.

But having a hunger isn't enough. Athletes and coaches must have something that drives and stokes the fire of hunger, keeping it burning.

Let's explore a few. As we mention each one, consider whether it is intrinsic or extrinsic:

1. **The desire to prove someone wrong**. Very often, players were told at an early age that it would be impossible for them to make a team or be successful in their sport. Some were cut from their team or counted out.

2. **The desire to prove someone right.** When someone believes in you – such as your parents or a coach – you want to prove their faith in you to be correct. It's a hunger to give something back to those individuals.

3. **The desire to prove something to yourself.** Many times, athletes and coaches personally question their own commitment to their sport. In doing so, they push themselves in an effort to show how much the game means to them and – in the process – accomplish bigger things.

4. **The desire to be at the top of your profession.** It may simply be that a coach or athlete's desire to become the champion or statistical leader in their respective sport enables them to do whatever is necessary.

5. **The desire to overcome an injury or hardship.** An injury can often cost an athlete their career. On the other hand, an athlete with hunger will decide to work as hard as possible to come back stronger than ever.

6. **Life challenge.** They may also have experienced hardship or a seemingly insurmountable challenge in life (poverty, the loss of a loved one, etc.) that drives their hunger to beat it through their sport at all costs.

7. **Their personality and DNA.** Some athletes are essentially born to be great. It's part of their DNA, and they're intrinsically driven to give everything they have.

They have that Type-A personality, totally focused, never letting anything or anyone get in their way.

8. **The desire to earn a reward.** Some athletes are driven by a scholarship, a trophy, a ring, a championship, or the adulation that goes with being successful. While this may work out for some, it is the easiest to walk away from. There simply isn't as much invested or deep-rooted hunger.

What does this have to do with *your* team? You may only want your players to work together toward a championship without a hunger for breaking individual records, and that's a great goal. But how can you build a hunger within that team for them to do more than necessary to get to a championship game? How can they understand or grasp that hunger? What can you do or say to paint a picture to encapsulate what hunger looks like?

Here are a few ideas:

1. **Individual hardships**. Find out what each player has given up, fought through, or lost in their career to this point. Have every player share with the rest of the team.

2. **Guest speaker**. Have someone who has sacrificed and fought through many challenges but kept going while accomplishing so much. Have your players come up with two questions beforehand to ask at the end of the presentation, as well as one that comes to mind as they listen.

3. **Helping the less privileged.** Take your team to a homeless shelter or hospital for children battling life-threatening illnesses and disabilities. Let them work or spend time volunteering there, getting to know the people personally and observing how hard they work.

4. **Showing what a championship looks like.** Have members of a state or national championship team visit with your team. What did they give up to accomplish the championship? What do they remember about the practices? Were there ever any doubts, arguments or disagreements?

5. **Who do you owe for your career?** Have your players research what their parents have given up for them to play. What were their parents' hopes and dreams? Let them share their findings with the team.
6. **What would you do for your teammates?** Have your players answer: What makes a great teammate? Why should I help my teammates? Think of your favorite teammate… what makes them special? Then, call on several players to share.
7. **Observing your parents and all they do for you.** Have your players list what they've seen their parents do to support the team and support them personally. Have them list what they've done for their parents in return.

Players' motivations for playing may vary, but what drives them every day to show up for practice, meetings and the game? Do they have a hunger? Many have never thought about it in such terms, but they should.

Through your leadership and guidance, they can see how important hunger is for accomplishing great things.

Here are three questions a player must answer before their journey.

1. Is it worth the effort required?
2. Am I willing to commit to that effort?
3. Will my coach be brave enough to tell me if my effort isn't enough?

Hunger is obvious in any walk of life or profession, or at tough times. Without it, we wander and have no direction or focus. Watch someone down on their luck, homeless, jobless or who has lost a loved one. The one who has a hunger to recover or make it through another day is easily spotted. They are relentless; they never give up and have a vision of where they want to be. Those same traits are obvious in an athlete or team driven by a hunger to win a game or a championship.

Paint a picture of hunger for your team. Have them recognize what it looks like, what it requires, and then turn them loose. There simply is no better motivation.

WHAT SETS YOUR TEAM APART?

I've always had a lot of pride in how our players conduct themselves on and off the field. Our coaches have always preached, "You represent yourself, your family, and your school in everything you do."

During the District Tournament a few years ago, our team played the second game, and arriving early, we found a place in the bleachers watching the game before us. It was a heated battle between our cross-town rival and the host school. As the game wore on, it became apparent that tensions and restraint were wearing thin. Suddenly, an ugly fight broke out, and several players from both teams joined the pile. Order was finally restored, and the game finished with our rival winning, but the damage had been done.

We also won our game that night, but it would mean a tough game against our rival. As we arrived for the championship game and walked through the gate, I asked which bench was ours. The person taking money proceeded to give me a verbal lesson in controlling my team, and what a disgrace the fight "we were in" was with respect to sportsmanship and family values. As he continued, I interrupted him and said, "That was the other school, not us." As he looked up, he said, "Oh", and muttered something else as we walked on. The assumption was that if we were from the same area, we must act and have the same team values as the team that was in the fight. Nothing could have been further from the truth.

So, what sets or will set your team apart?

Very simply, it's *you*, the coach.

Your team is a reflection of you, your expectations, your tone, your demeanor, your passion, your drive, and your personality. Certainly, there will be a time or two when something is out of your control, but for the most part, everything reflects your imprint on the team. The other coach in my story was a fiery guy who seemed to have a chip on his shoulder all the time, and his team played the same way. Is that bad? Not as long as it can be channeled in a positive way to achieve the desired results.

Let's look at factors that impact why players, fans, and other coaches will view your team differently.

1. **You keep or recruit the right players.** While it's safe to say you want the most skilled players possible, I believe you want players who have impeccable character, are responsible, trustworthy, and academically sound. When you combine those attributes with skill, you have players who can proudly represent your team in a positive way.

2. **You work to close skill gaps.** Having a skills program – whether off-season, before school, or after – will pay big dividends. Other coaches, parents, and fans will wonder how you get so many players who are so highly skilled, but you'll know how much work it takes and how important it is.

3. **You recognize and value each and every player.** Players need to know how much you and your staff recognize and value what they do in practice and games. That doesn't mean you have to have a party or celebrate every moment; just a word or two from time to time makes a huge difference in a player's outlook and demeanor.

4. **Your former players are better people by participating in the program.** When your former players have been part of something special, they will spread the word to everyone they meet. They become the leaders of your community and will always be the ambassadors for your program.

5. **Values and integrity are above winning and posturing.** You will inevitably be faced with a decision where winning and/or making the right decision by sitting someone out will be your options. It's a moment you'll have to live with for the rest of your life, and one your players will be watching closely. Always do the right thing, even when it's tough.

Reasons players will be glad they became a part of your program:

- Players are inspired by your team leaders and encouraged to lead as well.
- Decisions are made whenever possible in a shared manner with the team.
- Communication and feedback are crystal clear and timely.
- Expectations are built by the coaches and players.
- Coaches are open and listen to new ideas.
- Players' roles are clearly defined.
- Credit and rewards are always shared.
- Accountability is always present and expected by players and coaches.

In a world of many teams, take a moment and think: what sets your team apart? How important is that? You and others may not always see it game after game, but when moments are tough, or compassion is needed, it will be obvious what your team stands for and believes in. That will be the true measure of your impact on the team.

Lay the groundwork for what you want to see, and then let the team shine brightly to those who need to see it most. Because the thing that sets your team apart begins with *you*.

INSPIRATION

COMPASSION:
CAN YOU SHOW IT?

There may be a number of reasons why players walk away from your team. Can you control these factors? For some factors, the answer is yes; others might involve compromising what you believe is best for the team. When we talk about players harassing teammates in an effort to run them off, for example, that's an area you must control and eliminate. Those players doing the harassing are not the type of players you need on your team. While some players may leave your team because of your personality or playing time, that's a challenge the player (for the most part) will need to work through if they want to stay.

Each reason for leaving is unique and, in some small way, a time for the player to grow. They may have simply lost their love for the game and what it requires. In essence, priorities change. For others, working through the thought of quitting may rekindle their love for the game. As you think about your own career, at what point did you leave the game? Have you walked away from a job? As we move through life, there will be moments when we know it's time to leave.

But as we think about the player or players that left our team, have you ever had one want to come back after a short period, or the following season? It's pretty common. When a player has devoted their whole life to this point in the game, walking away is tough, especially if they associate with members of the team. How will you handle the question when they ask? How will you respond?

In my particular case, when I was playing, I thought all would be forgotten with an apology and I'd be at practice the next day. That wasn't going to happen. My coach told me to come back in a week, and he'd have an answer. As a young 10th grader, little did I know the coach was surveying the team, getting their input, talking with assistants, and thinking about how letting me back on the team might cause more harm than good.

When we finally met, he let me know how my selfish interests had let the team down and how my teammates would now view me differently – asking themselves if they could trust and count on this guy. As I held my head down and thought about it, his voice raised an octave and said, "Well, can they?" "Can I?"

I assured him it wouldn't happen again and, for a moment, wasn't sure if I was in or out. After a long silence, he looked me in the eye and said, "If it wasn't for our Assistant Coach, I wouldn't let you back. He really believes in you." I'm going to put you back on the team, but here are my conditions, and if you don't live up to them, you'll make my decision easy. You've lost all status on the team, won't be dressing out for any games for three weeks, and while the other players practice, you'll be running 100 laps – including the bleachers – without a break.

For the next three weeks, I wondered if it was really worth it, argued with myself, hated the coach, and vowed he wouldn't break me. My determination was greater than ever. As my reward, I was going to make the starting lineup; it didn't matter who was in my way. Sitting on the bench wasn't where I wanted to be, and I never planned to be there again. And yes, I did earn that spot in the starting lineup for the rest of my career, earning a scholarship to play at the next level.

Bringing a player back is never easy; there are so many dynamics to consider. What will the team think? Will it disrupt our chemistry? Am I doing it just because they're a great player? What if it happens again? Will it be used against me by other players who need to be held accountable? What conditions must be met to be able to come back? Why did they quit in the first place? What has changed?

In my case, I believe the coach handled it in the right manner. Not because he gave me a second chance but because of the circumstances.

1. He surveyed or talked with the team.
2. There was no malice or ill intent on my part toward teammates or coaches; if there had been, I should not have been allowed back.
3. A coach stood up for me at a time that would change my life.

4. Conditions were set and clearly had to be followed to come back.
5. The question of how badly this player wanted to be back on the team was answered with a vengeance.

No coach or experience can tell you whether it's right to bring a player back. You lay yourself on the line and – when you do – you risk the possibility of losing a lot of respect from your team if it goes bad. Is one young person's career worth it? At the time I needed it most after making a terrible decision, a coach stood up for and believed in me. A thank you I'll never be able to repay and a life lesson carried with me every day.

IF IT WAS JUST COACHING, IT'D BE EASY!

Have you ever said, "If it was just coaching, it'd be easy!" Most coaches have said just that – at some point in their careers – after being loaded down and burdened with situations they never expected when they entered the profession. Paperwork, scheduling, cancellations, meetings, injuries, eligibility, recruiting, parent concerns, and team dynamics can take up much of your time. So, how can you do it all while still having time to prepare your team for the season and the next game?

If you're a detail person, it may be a little easier, but if not, it can take some work.

These may help:

1. **Delegate to assistants.** Anything that doesn't require the head coach to be in attendance can be handled by your assistants. Give them the responsibility of representing you and the team in certain situations. If they aspire to be a head coach, they need the experience you can offer.
2. **Budget your time.** Designate specific times of the day and/or week for meeting with administrators, parents, fundraisers, or anyone else that might take you away from your team. Let those people know when they can see you. If they call or contact you, set the date and time that works best for you.
3. **Earlier versus later.** Develop a habit of coming into work early to take care of paperwork, entering stats, etc., before anyone can bother you. Putting it off until the end of the day or after the game will be tough, considering you're mentally tired and not as sharp. Time alone allows you to do a better job, and it gives you time to think clearly about other pressing matters as well.
4. **Do it now.** If you promised to have something completed today, get it done. Tomorrow will present you with challenges you hadn't planned on. Those you work for

need to know they can count on you with respect to deadlines.

5. **Never sacrifice the team.** Your players count on you. Always be at practice and the game, and travel with them unless it's an emergency. Catching up on something at the expense of the team will cost you more than you could ever imagine. If you expect them to be there, shouldn't you also?

6. **Focus on family.** Time taken away in the evening from the family for work you could have done that day will never be replaced. Coaching takes away enough time with games and travel, so embrace those family opportunities when it doesn't. Your family is more important than your job. If you choose to sacrifice something, do it so you can spend time with them.

7. **Plan/plan/plan.** Develop a template of plans in the off-season with your staff for travel, practice, events, and more for the *entire* season. Plans may change during the year, but you'll have blueprints to work with that will minimize periods of adjustment. In doing this, issues that require more time won't interfere with anything else.

8. **Team leaders.** Designated team leaders can assist you with areas related specifically to team dynamics, ideas, and planning related to senior night, banquets, travel, etc. Their involvement gives them a true sense of leading the team and builds their leadership skills. You'll see another side of these leaders and be amazed when they say, "Relax, coach. We can handle this."

9. **Team parents.** If you have a booster or parent organization, let them handle all the fundraising, pre-game and post-game meals, picture day, setting up the field, and other activities while on the road. Parents want to feel a part of the team and contribute to their child's sports experience. Trusting their decisions in a shared leadership situation with you will help the team and reduce your workload.

There will be days when you feel overwhelmed by everything you're faced with. The key is to share the load with those you trust, such as your assistants, players, and often your Athletic Director. When you build a solid relationship with them, they're more than willing to help in any way possible.

By being a proactive coach, you can give full attention to the one area that needs you most – your team!

INSPIRATIONAL WORDS

Have you ever wondered why that end-of-the-season speech (down to possibly your last fixture's pregame speech) seems to carry more weight and influence than any others during the regular season? After all, that game against the #1 team in the state to begin the year was pretty important, and how about that game against your cross-town rival?

I am pretty sure we'd agree that it has as much to do with our audience – in this case, our players – as anything else. Players who sense this could be their last game usually rise as high as possible to play their best, and often we forget that, thinking it was our pregame speech that motivated them. That could be the case, but let's think about what's involved with our words.

Tournament speeches are usually the easiest. Why? Because they're authentic and real to you and your players. Players have a vision of what it might look like if the season ends tonight, and your words come from the heart and are genuine.

So, the question begs, "How can we make that impact every time we speak?" Honestly, I'm not sure that's always possible, but it may be if we consider all the ingredients of a message that will resonate long after our game is over and your player's careers have ended.

Here are some ingredients to consider to help your words come to life and make them meaningful when players need them most.

1. **Make it special.** Avoid using a speech after every practice, every workout, every team meeting. Your words should have meaning, and the players should be hoping for that 'moment', knowing you don't waste them on just any daily routine.

2. **Heartfelt and Genuine.** Nothing comes more naturally or has more meaning than words at key moments, such as a possible last game, the death of one of your player's relatives, or a season-ending injury. However, it doesn't mean those are the only moments. Sometimes, the

emotion runs high as you share your thoughts with your players. Those moments will never be forgotten.

3. **Lead Them to Remember.** Have your players close their eyes and reflect on that first day they joined the program, met their teammates, and smiled with joy. What do they see? How does it make them feel?

4. **Hopes and Dreams.** What hopes and dreams did they have when they became a part of the program? What have they accomplished? What is still yet to be completed?

5. **Sacrifice.** Remind your players of the hours they've dedicated to your team. Think about what they've sacrificed to be here. What have they given up? How many hours have they put into the team's success?

6. **Look around.** Consider all the teammates that the players have counted on, and continue to count on, not just for the games and practice but for their friendship and kind words in tough moments.

7. **All we have is tonight.** This is the time they've waited and worked for all season. It's their time to shine. They've earned the right to be here, so show their opponent what this team and these players are made of and leave it all on the field.

8. **Personal.** "I've watched and witnessed each one of you deal with and work through tough times on and off the field. That allows me to be a pretty good judge of who you really are, and what you are capable of. As you think of some of those moments, it will give you strength and courage in this game tonight. Let no one stand in your way."

9. **Vision of success.** "Close your eyes and relax your mind. Think and see what it will look like when you are successful tonight. That feeling of adulation after a game where you gave all you had. Can you see your parents, your friends? What are they doing? Now, open your eyes and see the opportunity in front of you. It's time; turn that vision into a reality."

10. **Proud of you.** "I believe in each one of you. I am so proud to be your coach. We've worked through some challenges, but it allowed us to better understand each other, and I will always be grateful for what you taught me. My life has been blessed by everything you brought to our team."

I know, personally, there were times when I struggled to find words to help my team be successful or win a game. As coaches, we want to do all we can to help our players. That can mean spending a lot of time trying to craft a pregame speech that can magically transform our team into something it may not be. That doesn't mean we will work any less, but we must realize that for those words to even have a chance, they must reach into every player's heart and soul. They must have more meaning than a rah! rah! speech that usually only lasts for two or three minutes into the game.

If you want to know what gets your players' attention, what their priorities are, and what means the most to them… ask them! Have a classroom session defining and refining their top ten. This may give you insight into reaching your players with certain ingredients in your pregame speeches, as well as assisting you in practice and during games.

Understand that when a pregame speech impacts every player, it rides with them the whole game and (maybe more importantly) the rest of their life. As important as that game may have been, it's over, but their journey in life is just beginning.

MOTIVATION: WHERE DO YOU FIND IT?

Do you have video clips or audio files downloaded, plus quotes and material, that you draw from for personal motivation? How long do they last? Do you refer to notes or things you've written down to pull up key phrases and words at crucial times?

There are many sources of inspiration out there. But when you come to deploy them with your team, do they come from the heart, allowing you to connect better with your players? What *exactly* are we searching for when we scroll for the right words, the right phrase, or the right message for ourselves during challenging times or before a game?

I think you would agree that we spend a lot of time and money searching for the perfect motivation from those who may have never been in our shoes, to either help us with our coaching ability and performance, or to assist our team achieve greatness in a game or a season. Motivation seems to be all around us and easily accessed. But do you find that outside motivation wears off when you return to what you know is true: your own experiences, your heartfelt values, or what those you hold in high esteem have taught you over the years?

So, what is the key to motivation? When you break motivation down, it's words from a quote, a spirited speech, or someone who has battled adversity with a real-life message. So, how can we make that motivation last? It all has to do with looking in the mirror every day, repeating the message, making sure we follow through, and holding the motivation close. Simply put, motivation only works if we (or those our message is intended to reach) truly believe it and turn it into action.

We often draw our motivation from conventions, seminars, and meetings where a motivational speaker is present. Coaches are sometimes skeptical, and just by being there – in person – we get a glimpse of how real the speaker is, and a sense of their sincerity. The fact that we can talk with them after their presentation also lends credibility to their value in our eyes. Therefore, we're more willing to purchase their product and buy into their words in a book or other material.

When you consider all the motivational moments you've experienced in your career, I think you'd agree that motivation rarely is often fleeting. It's what we've learned through personal experience – such as an unpleasant confrontation, the loss of a loved one, winning a championship, being fired, an unexpected thank you, a decision you knew was wrong, or a player who went on to greatness – that really stays with us and fuels our motivation.

We want personal motivation to be full of positives and a wonderful outlook, but as you know, it can be those times we make a mistake, or something goes wrong, that motivates us to become better and strive to learn from that situation.

I believe there are six questions you can ask to really embrace motivation, and for it to have the power to last in your career. Here are those six questions:

1. What are your motives for coaching?
2. What do you want to accomplish?
3. What do you stand for?
4. What is most important in your personal life?
5. What are the strengs of your personality?
6. What feeds your ability to be impactful?

Coaching hinges on your motives. What do you want to accomplish, and would you do anything to get there, even if it's not right? What do you stand for? Can you say 'enough is enough' when you see a wrong? Is your personality sincere to what is best for your players?

Motivation isn't a quote, a speech, a book, or a presentation. It's the vocation you've chosen. Every day, your players look to you for motivation. It need not be over the top or from a book; it just needs to be sincere, honest, and from the heart.

THE MOTIVATION IS YOU.

PLAYERS' MIXED MESSAGES

How do you work with a player who must continually be reminded to do a task, strategy, or skill in practice; or play a game with effort, intensity, and commitment? I know coaches, regardless of status, won/lost records, or accomplishments, who have been frustrated at imploring players to do things a certain way. They plead with them to work harder or take the game more seriously. Surprisingly (or maybe not), the players we are talking about can potentially become your best players.

Frustration stems from thoughts of 'What *are* they thinking?' Indeed, "I've told them specifically, every day for the last two weeks, to play the ball wide, play the ball through, or take the defender on with intensity at practice or in a game. Why is this still a problem?" We start out by giving players the benefit of the doubt (maybe they didn't understand what we wanted), so we explain what we're seeing – and what we need – for the umpteenth time. However, it's not long until old habits reappear.

Our next thought may be that they don't have a mental picture of what we need. After painting it in detail, we feel better and send them back to practice or the game, only to see the same issue. At that point, we have often had enough.

Until we find a solution or answer, our options are: place them with an assistant coach to clarify and correct the problem, sit them out, pull them from the game, or send them to the locker room.

What could possibly be going on here? This happened more than once in my career, and I've witnessed it as a college assistant as well. When I've met with players, they would say, "My Mom/Dad told me to do it this way," or "My club coach said it's better if you play this way."

I'm not here to bash parents or other coaches; they have their own ideas, styles of play, and knowledge of the game. If they want a player in their season to play a certain way to help their team, it's their prerogative.

It becomes confusing when players are getting mixed messages from other sources. When they play for you, players need to know unequivocally that this is what you expect and need from them, regardless of what they do for their club team or even what mom or dad expect.

There may be one other area you may not have considered. One of your assistant coaches, for example. An assistant may have innocently tried to help a player and pushed them in the wrong direction. It could also be that a player manipulated the assistant, so they have an excuse when you confront them. Young coaches fall into this trap frequently when they become an assistant with their team. Their playing days have recently ended, and they don't yet have the experience to see the problem. Be aware that some players will use that friendship in a selfish way to take liberties at practice or in a game. Make certain you discuss these potential issues with new assistants.

We also need to look in the mirror. As the head coach, could *we* be the culprit? Think for a moment… are your messages or directions always crystal clear? I have, at times, stopped an activity in practice because it resembles nothing like I thought it would when I put it together. Rather than get frustrated, I usually laugh a little and apologize, then explain – in better terms – what I expect with clearer instructions. Anything after that, for the most part, is on the players.

How about in a game? Can players really hear you on the sidelines? Do they have time to listen while the play continues? Are they being belligerent when they don't respond? Most of the time, the play is over when we yell what they *should* have done. Is that helping? Will we become upset if it happens again? Should we have covered it in practice?

What about phrases we might use in a game, such as unlucky, work hard, keep grinding, one more, good job, wider, make a run. Phrases are great if players understand them and know what to do next. However, they can be a mixed message when they're not specific and – more importantly – there's no direction or solution. We can cover all considerations in practice, before the game, halftime, on the sideline, or after the game.

With respect to parents, what will we do when their voice is louder than ours? Sometimes, we notice our player looking in the stands and listening to their family members during a game. Parents should always be considered an asset *until they're not*. It's important we explain – at the preseason meeting – our expectations for their son or daughter and ask them to trust our decisions.

Remind parents that they can contact us to set up a meeting if they feel it's needed. Explain your philosophy with respect to always doing what's best for the team, our emphasis on developing character and integrity, and providing an encouraging, challenging, and positive environment for them to grow and develop.

How can you decrease mixed messages?

1. Players always need to tune into our radio station 98.1, or whatever metaphor you decide, at practice and the game. They can listen to other stations, such as mom or dad or other influences, on their own time.

2. Come up with a way to communicate with players in a game that doesn't reduce their focus. The keys are timing, minimal words, and no negatives.

3. Corrections can also be made at halftime or by taking the player out.

4. Players should relay back and confirm to parents what we expect from them.

5. Do your best in practice and games to paint a picture of what you expect from players. Anything less, stop it at practice or get them out of the game.

6. Train your assistant coaches and team leaders to ask questions or make statements to teammates that define the team, such as:

   - "As a defender, tell me what you'd do in numbers down, 1 v 2 coming right at you?"

   - "As an attacker, when will you decide to take a defender on?"

   - "As a center midfielder, what are you looking for with the ball at your feet?"

- "We don't play that way here. Our game plan is…"

- "If you're not going to give 110%, this may not be the team for you."

- "I've seen you work; I know how fast and skilled you can be."

- "Come on, we need you! Make that diagonal run one more time."

Mixed messages aren't something new, and they can originate anywhere: from friends, even well-meaning teachers, youth ministers, or relatives. Players simply don't want to disappoint, and when someone gets in their ear, it influences their ability to play (especially young players) – usually in a negative way – because they're trying to do more than possible.

There's no way to keep players from hearing those messages. It's important to explain how to deal with them. Keep in mind they see these people just about every day, so they feel accountable. They know they'll be asked *why* they didn't do what was asked, or applauded for what they did do. For younger players, it's a heavy burden.

For older players, it can be a real dilemma, signaling the player may have essentially tuned us out and has more respect for someone else's opinion or ideas. That's a situation that must be resolved in a timely manner. Remember, it's not about power or control, although we may see it that way. It's about convincing and reminding the player of their role on your team. In the end, though, it will be our decision to live with it or not. I can assure you, it won't get any better without strong leadership on your part.

Keep building rapport with your players. Remind them every day that their number one responsibility on your team is their teammates. Our message must be crystal clear, without interference, and the most important one they hear. Keep the radio loud and clear as they listen.

SELF-DISCIPLINE

I like to define self-discipline as an overlooked, underappreciated, and often unrecognized trait applied by coaches and/or players when words, demeanor, or actions are suppressed, as they would stand to inflame a situation.

When's the last time you thought of saying something, caught yourself, and decided it probably wouldn't be a good idea at that moment? If you're like me, it happens every day, especially with others sharing ideas and thoughts on social media which you disagree with, or feel are incorrect. It takes a lot just to let it go.

How about in your coaching career? At some point, I'm sure you've been confronted or asked about a game decision, playing time, or an award by a parent who felt their child was slighted. How did you react? Did you try to convince parents of the merit of your decision? Did you go into detail about their son or daughter's deficiencies and lack of talent? Did it help or make the situation worse?

I believe you'd agree that you will never convince parents to change their minds in certain situations. In many cases, they will never join you in your assessment of their child. With that in mind, applying self-discipline and an appropriate demeanor in your conversation may be best at this time. It does no good to list what this player can't do; it only inflames the parents, even if you know it to be true.

How about with officials? How often have you had a call reversed while yelling and screaming at an official? Is it helping your team? I know a lot of coaches feel it will help on the next call, but do we know that for sure? It could work quite the opposite when an official now appears to be leaning against you and your team. I'm certainly not against you making a point when your team is slighted; it's just the way you do it.

What about your players? Do they often see you out of control on the sideline and think it's okay for them to do the same in the game? Are you teaching them self-discipline? If you've witnessed an out-of-control team on the field, you typically look no farther than the bench to see where it originates. You'll see an out-of-control coach with little to no self-discipline, teaching his or her players to act the same way.

I admit that it's tough to remain in control and say nothing during moments of a game or when standing in front of an angry parent; it is human nature to think about all the things you *could* say. Self-discipline isn't easy, and there may be a time or two you must let go. We must remember who's watching us – our players – and make a point to talk about it with them. Reminding them it isn't the norm, but there will be times when you have to stand up and say what needs to be said.

Let's keep in mind it doesn't always mean a situation is controversial or confrontational. It could be something you know in strict confidence that should not be shared. You might be momentarily motivated to share it but decide not to because it might impact someone or worsen a situation.

Players need to apply self-discipline every day. By being a part of the team, every word and action reflects what your team stands for. I often use the phrase, "We all wear the same jersey." Reminding them to exercise self-discipline while fellow students are partying, staying up late, eating anything they want, and saying anything on social media posts, is a big challenge for players to contend with. While they need to "know" these things, they urgently need to be "taught" self-discipline not only in the classroom but by your example of words, actions, and how you live and coach.

I'm reminded of a story about President Abraham Lincoln, who was visiting the troops during the Civil War. As he entered the tent of one of his generals, he noticed the general was penning a letter with a sense of fervor and urgency. When he asked the general who the letter was intended for, he replied, "It's to another general who has aggrieved me through his words about my command." Lincoln asked to see the letter and, upon reading it, looked at the general and said, "You really told him," before he scrunched it up and threw it in the trash basket. Has anyone ever convinced you not to say what you have on your mind? Have you used self-discipline by deleting a potential post or tweet after thinking about it for a moment? It's a great example of modeling self-discipline by getting it out of your system.

One of our greatest battles may be feeling we have to voice our opinion or stance when confronted or challenged. When it happens, we often respond without listening, failing to acknowledge the other person or their point of view. This often causes the situation to escalate by using words that can never be taken back. Is that the solution we want? What has your experience taught you? What did you learn from your coaches, teachers, or parents?

A couple of phrases we've all heard are, "Stand up for yourself" and "Don't let someone walk all over you." Does that apply all the time? Can we step outside the moment in our mind and see it from the other side? Will we be able to say we were wrong – if it's true – before the conversation ends? What exactly are we trying to prove? That we know more than the other person, we're the expert, or that we are always, right?

When we use self-discipline not to win but to understand, it allows us to take a breath and not feel threatened. Listening becomes easier when we aren't searching for the right answer or justification. Just by being silent, we allow the other person to voice their frustrations, even if we don't totally agree. Maybe, just maybe, being heard is all they wanted anyway.

Self-discipline is, in itself, disarming. It feels surreal, like you're a third person who is invisible and listening to the complaint or issue. There will be challenges with players and parents you must deal with; it's part of coaching. Self-discipline through listening doesn't mean you necessarily agree, though. It means you're in control of your emotions and words, allowing you to make the best decisions possible. It's not always easy, but in the end, we gain a lot more than we lose.

Watch coaches and players who've mastered self-discipline on the sideline and in a game. They understand that to be in control, they must remain calm and mentally under control to help their team best. They see more than a bad call by an official, a missed shot, a shove by an opponent, or verbal outbursts from the opposing bench. They see the next play. Controversies are ignored; they mean nothing in the quest to be successful. It's wasted energy and time to think about them or dwell on them. I know you've thought, "How in the world can they be so calm?" but individuals with self-discipline see what anger, harsh words, and being upset can never see. They see the opportunities for the next play and realize it needs no words or wasted emotions. These coaches and players realize they lose their ability to think clearly when emotions take over. Embrace "self-discipline." Teach it to your players in every situation, in the classroom, and all you do and say. They'll need it long after they leave your team.

THAT LAST LOSS... DO MY PLAYERS CARE?

As a coach, think back to that *one particular loss* that still lingers in your mind. Heartbreaking, everything given, you just had to stand in front of your team and let them know how proud you are of their efforts and the unbelievable season they've had. That loss robs you of every ounce of energy at that moment, and you can barely sleep that night. Indeed, you keep reliving the match for days, thinking of every "what if" you can imagine, and putting all the responsibility on yourself.

Sound familiar? If you've coached for any period, you've had an experience close to or like this. But how do the players deal with it? Often, we see them leaving the field and talking with their friends or teammates as if nothing happened. At school the next day, it's as if they flipped a switch off and activated some wholly new mode that comes with no remorse. How can that be!?

As a coach, I'm not sure our outlook will ever change. We hold ourselves responsible, so in every case where we aren't successful, we go back to "What could I have done?" And, in some cases, that involves big tournament games that haunt us forever.

Have you ever been bothered by how little it seems to mean to some of your players? It's natural. Should we hope they feel as bad as we do? Would that help or change the outcome? Never.

Here are a few reasons why our players seem to deal with these moments better than we do:

1. **Youth.** Young people will always be more resilient than adults. They're able to let a moment go and move on much more quickly. That doesn't mean something wasn't tough on them; they just learn and let it go, unlike some of us.
2. **Other interests/sports.** As a coach, you usually coach one sport, so think about it. All your focus is on that sport. It's your career and what you put your heart and soul into. Young players, however, often have many other interests and friends, and may play other sports. For them, the end

of one season isn't the end of the world, it's just time to move to the next sport or outside interest.

3. **Not personal.** Many players understand and embrace a team game where the joy or sadness is shared by all for a small moment, and then it's time to move on. If it's one player's mistake that cost the game, will that particular player hold onto it and be upset for an extended period?

4. **Control their emotions.** Some players refuse to show their emotions in tough situations because they've been taught to believe it's a sign of weakness. Again, it doesn't mean it doesn't hurt; it's just their way of dealing with the loss.

5. **Family support/values.** Players who are brought up in a very supportive family understand their value isn't based on winning and being successful every time they play. When at home, they know they will hear messages of encouragement that reaffirm all they've accomplished.

6. **Positive self-worth/self-image.** At the end of the day, your players play your sport and give it all they have, but when they look in the mirror, they don't see it as defining who they are, what they represent, or how they are viewed. To them, it's just a part of their life.

7. **Personality.** It could be that certain players aren't accustomed to or comfortable in sharing their feelings of disappointment in front of you or their peers. They may think it hurts their status or friendships within the team, and they'd rather deal with this by themselves.

I must admit there have been a few times in my career when I couldn't understand how some of my players weren't more upset by a loss that meant so much to our team and our program. I was a little jealous as I watched some of them head off with gear in hand to greet their friends, smiling and talking as they walked to the parking lot. It was as if nothing had happened.

"If only I could let it go that easy," I thought.

Later, I wondered at what point those apparently carefree players would feel real disappointment with a loss as big as this one. Then

I realized, do you *have* to feel bad in every loss? How exactly does that help?

Players will always deal with losing in different ways. Some are recognizable, while others may be very different from our point of view. That doesn't mean the loss didn't hurt them; they just know the sun will shine tomorrow, their friends will still care about them, and their life is consumed by a lot of great things.

Our pain and disappointment will always be greater and often obvious. Many times, we carry it around like dragging an anchor everywhere we go, thinking everyone knows about our loss. I hate to disappoint you, but there are many who have no idea or real concern about you or your team. While that may seem harsh, it's true. Just remember, no one is going to feel sorry for you, and yes, your players feel it as well. Let it go and move on!

Just be glad you have another chance to coach again next week or next season.

INTEGRITY

ASKING TOUGH QUESTIONS...
OF OURSELVES

There are many forms out there that enable us to evaluate our players. In turn, there's the one our ADs use to evaluate us.

Have you ever spent time thinking what an evaluation form for yourself would look like if *you* developed it? Not necessarily for the past season, but one that also covered where your program is today, the direction it's headed, and your coaching performance. You may have said to yourself during routine evaluations, "I could come up with better questions than that!"

Could you be objective in the criteria? Could you be completely honest in your answers?

No one is tougher on us than ourselves when we're passionate, committed, and dedicated to our team. We've all spent nights asking "why" and "how" when our team wasn't successful or was uncharacteristically mistake-prone. While some coaches may not have the resources or experience to generate ideas designed to improve their weaknesses or expand their strengths, who knows better what those weaknesses or strengths are?

Let's look at some questions we might consider when we look in the mirror.

1. What is my level of commitment and dedication to our team?
2. What did my players learn from me in a loss? A win?
3. Am I strong enough to trust my players in key situations?
4. Does my program have a philosophy of shared leadership?
5. What is one area that needs immediate attention?
6. Are my players free to share their ideas or suggestions?
7. Am I spending adequate time preparing for practice?
8. Is my demeanor on the sideline constructive/controlled?
9. Do I berate a player immediately after a mistake?
10. What is my level of enthusiasm?
11. Did I take the time to meet and talk with players who didn't make our team?

12. Am I a positive role model on and off the field?
13. Do I mention and highlight one or more role players to the media?
14. Was I gracious in my remarks when asked about our opponent?
15. What meaningful roles do my assistants have? Am I training them to be a head coach?
16. Do I overuse nonspecific comments such as: Good job! Great idea! Unlucky!
17. How well do I communicate with my Athletic Director?
18. Am I delegating responsibilities to my assistants and team leaders?
19. Do I have a system for dealing with player challenges outside the game?
20. Am I consistently holding players accountable?
21. How would I rate my character and integrity?
22. Am I brief when making a point in a teachable moment?
23. Can I be humble in a win and gracious in a loss?
24. Do I represent our players at state/national award meetings?
25. Is my decision-making consistent?
26. Am I involved in coach education?
27. Did I visit with officials before the game this season?
28. What was our level of success this season? How is it defined?
29. What are my plans for our team next year?
30. Do I always look in the mirror first in times of crisis?
31. What is one incident this year that I wish I'd handled differently?
32. From delegation, enthusiasm, character, planning, teaching, trust, communication, and game situations, which two are my strongest? Which two need work?
33. Did I deflect blame from our players for a loss this season to myself?
34. Does our team have a list of expectations?
35. Was I completely honest with players concerning their roles?
36. Can I talk to our team in a heartfelt, sincere manner?

37. Did I do my best to thank those who work behind the scenes?
38. Am I building a program or just planning season to season?
39. Did I meet with parents before the season?
40. Do I contact teachers with respect to players' conduct, schoolwork, and responsibilities?
41. Am I challenging players to take their game to a higher level?
42. Did I involve our players in community projects?
43. Did I provide leadership classes or team-building activities for our team?
44. Do I know the talents/skills our players have outside our game?
45. Do I only teach when mistakes are made?
46. Did I pitch in and help with fundraising activities?
47. Would I consider myself a good listener? Why or why not?

It's impossible to have a perfect score on all questions, but it shouldn't deter us from striving to be the best coach we can become. There will be times when we act out of character when asked about an incident that may have led to a loss. It happens. Recognizing it and using it as a learning tool is imperative. The important part is that we – as coaches – come up with our own questions that allow us to grow and evaluate our performance.

As we continue our careers, the questions will continue to pop up. It's our way of checking the GPS to see if we're headed in the right direction.

It's not always about the challenges we face; there are many questions when our season is a success as well. By looking in the mirror, we face our toughest critic, the one who doesn't allow us to relax, and always says, "You can do it; you're on the right track; don't give up."

BUILDING A TEAM CULTURE

Team culture continues to be a hot topic with everyone who wants to offer a view on 'what makes a team successful'. That said, I guess I'm no different(!) as I share what I consider to be important ideas for you to consider as you build your program. Most come from experience and – ultimately – what worked for me. Like anything else, if you can use or consider one or more, I've done my job.

It goes without saying that the culture of teams varies greatly and often leans heavily on the personality and style of the head coach. That can be a plus, allowing us to deal with certain challenges and issues in a way that utilizes our coaching principles, what we believe, and what we feel comfortable with. From a negative standpoint, though, it may keep us from reaching those players who don't share or agree with our philosophy. Is that wrong of them?

What do we do with those players? Keep them on the bench, cut them, or continue tolerating them? I'm certain it has happened, but is it the right thing to do? Should our philosophy or team culture guidelines incorporate flexibility, openness, and a willingness to listen to varying ideas and suggestions?

With the above in mind, how do we come up with areas for building our team culture? Do you have them laid out before your team is formed or arrives? Should you include the players in the process of determining your components, what gets included, and how they are defined? I believe so.

One of my big priorities is players taking ownership of every aspect of the team. That doesn't mean everything will be rosy and we will always agree, but when the players embrace the program, you'll find them taking care of challenges and issues that you've always dealt with (sometimes for years). Their effort at practice and games will be greatly increased. Their demeanor will be bright and receptive, and they will be willing to suggest new ideas for practice and outside activities.

Here are 15 components to consider for building your team's culture. My hope is that you are already using many of them, and if not, that at least one or two will gain your consideration.

1. **Be the example you want to see.** Lead with positive, encouraging, and challenging language.
2. **Empower and assist players.** Lead, guide, and trust players through leadership sessions as they teach one another.
3. **Teach players the art of questioning and listening.** No other attribute is as valuable as conversations with teammates.
4. **Develop expectations with the team.** Have a process where players voice expectations, offer their reasoning, and make decisions by narrowing down which ones to use for the season. You may have to add or suggest some if players haven't covered key concerns.
5. **Stamp "We" on all you do and say.** Use "We" every chance you get. Stay away from Me or I. Suggest the team create a symbol or reminder of WE.
6. **Lean into your team's talent. Learn to pull rather than push.** Pull the team's talents and abilities out to solve challenges and lead. Remind them of how much you believe in them, and what they are capable of.
7. **Create belonging.** Every player has a role, and is vitally important. Let them know that at every opportunity. Teach them that belonging also means they are part of something bigger than themselves, and ultimately responsible to every teammate.
8. **Foster mutual respect by being open, flexible, and receptive to new ideas.** Work with players who seem to be reluctant, apprehensive, or rebellious. Ask questions and listen as you consider a plan to assist them.
9. **Communicate clearly.** Leave no doubt or ambiguity about what you expect, what you believe in, and the decisions that must be made when accountability is necessary.
10. **Be vulnerable.** Be open and honest. If you make a mistake, or are wrong, admit it and move on. Incorporate

integrity into every decision and all you say and do. Always do the right thing for the right reason.

11. **Share responsibilities.** Allow players to assume certain responsibilities. Remind them that every aspect of the team is important, and many count on their willingness to serve the team.

12. **Determine a clear direction with the team.** Work with the team on setting goals for the season, as well as checkpoints along the way to monitor their progress.

13. **Provide opportunities for players to build team culture.** This might include team building, lunches, outside activities, and charities.

14. **Recognize positive and determined players and moments.** Get the team to create recognition symbols for practice, outside service, great teammates, games, etc.

15. **Bring a problem, bring a solution**. A great idea brought to me by a former player. It's easy to bring a problem to the coach or team leader, but can a player also bring a possible solution?

Team culture becomes a stamp you put on your program. It becomes the face of your program as well, in tough moments, joyous moments, and the everyday challenges you and your players face. Keep in mind that culture is a living, breathing example of everything your program stands for, and it is always a work in progress. You will need to learn from every situation and adjust when necessary.

Will your culture be easily defined by your actions and those of your players? Will it be positive or less than positive? If less than positive, maybe we can go back to our standards and re-evaluate. Just keep in mind that you and your players represent yourself, your school, and your family. While there will be challenges, I know you want your program to shine in the most positive light ever.

COACHING VULNERABILITY

Vulnerability. Not a word many coaches embrace. Often, we use it when talking about an opponent's weaknesses, such as they're vulnerable to a counterattack or they expose their vulnerability on corners by man-marking every time. And, in our coaching meetings, we may talk about *our* team's vulnerability in the next game. So, the impression and mental image is one of an advantage for our team or a weakness our opponent might expose.

But what about as a coach? How can vulnerability make us stronger? After all, we don't want a word associated with weakness being a part of our coaching style with our players. How could being vulnerable help us with our team? It will only make us appear weak and who would want to play for a weak, vulnerable coach? What other thoughts come to mind when you consider coaching vulnerability? What image of a vulnerable coach do you have at this moment?

Let's think about the definition as it pertains to our profession. It's a weakness or some area where we are exposed or at a perceived risk. Ideally, we always want to deal from a position of strength and confidence, but can being vulnerable help us lead our team? Will we know every answer for every situation?

Greg Popovich, five-time NBA championship coach with the San Antonio Spurs, gives us some insight into vulnerability with this quote, "Sometimes, in timeouts, I'll say, I've got nothing for you. What do you want me to do? We just turned the ball over six times. Everyone's holding the ball. What else do you want me to do here? Figure it out." Here, Popovich is doing his best to convince his players to lead themselves and, in the process, exposing his vulnerability to allow them to lead. Is it easy for you to let your players lead?

Vulnerability is a sign of courage and strength. You may not feel that way now, but letting others know you don't have all the answers – and you need their help – brings your team together and makes it stronger.

Think back on times you've felt vulnerable. That first day with a new team, that first game, the first day of school, meeting a new teammate, or that first day of class when you hoped you wouldn't be called on for answers.

In a more classic sense, feeling vulnerable may be, "What will I say after that heartbreaking loss?" "What do I say to my player who just tore her ACL?" "What do I tell my team after I made that bad decision?" "How will I explain that my player won't be starting tonight?" All these questions might require courageous answers; listening to the answers might not be what we want to hear.

When we think of connecting with our players, we want to be sincere, genuine, and authentic. It's what builds trust. It does no good to coach from a seemingly lofty position with a demeanor of I know every answer to every situation. When you do, it exiles your players to a lowly status and an environment that lacks sincerity, genuineness, and authenticity. It's only natural to want to know all the answers, but it may be better to say, "I don't know. Let's work together to find the answer."

We also feel vulnerable when players fill out the end-of-year surveys concerning the season and rating our coaching ability. It is not easy to read some of the comments, knowing you poured your heart and soul into the season. Sometimes, it is hard not to be somewhat upset. The same can be true when our Athletic Director evaluates our performance. Think of it this way, though, (and to repeat myself) *none of us are perfect or know all the answers*, so do your best to use feedback as a learning tool to grow and develop. If it helps, remember that you're not going to make every player happy.

Have you given thought about how vulnerability impacts your players? What signs have you noticed? How did you react? Have you had a player who was a perfectionist? Did it impact their ability to practice and play? A lot of our players grew up being praised for every statistical category in the game. It became the reason they played and how they (and others) evaluated their so-called success. Now, they play for your team, and if things don't go their way, they become their worst enemy. At this point, what can you do? Talk with them about vulnerability, using examples of previous players who finally realized they could be successful and still make mistakes.

Remind them their worth isn't based on numbers, and being vulnerable is about being courageous when the game doesn't always conform to our standards and expectations. Let them know that – by working together – you'll help them through the tough times.

For some coaches, it's all about having power. The power of being in charge, making all the decisions, having all the answers, being upfront, leading all the meetings, and talking to the media. In essence, it's all about them. It's their team, and in their mind, they're the reason the team is successful, or so they think. But vulnerability catches up with all of us if we don't embrace it. It's at that moment… when you're searching for the right answer without success, you're laboring over a decision you never made, or you can't help your team overcome a game-changing situation you've never seen. You have two choices. Make up an answer or solution that may not help or that you doubt, or ask your team what *they* feel would be a good solution. They know when you really don't know, so go ahead and let them figure it out. The power in this situation is working together.

Whether we admit it or not, we are vulnerable the moment we become a coach. There will be many situations we've never encountered before or know the solution to. Even after years of coaching, that doesn't change. Being vulnerable means you are open and honest with your players and seek to include them when searching for answers and solving problems along the way. In my best words to my players, it means I couldn't do this without you, and I wouldn't want to.

When we think back on what Coach Popovich shared, we get a glimpse of what can help us in vulnerable moments. And it's pretty simple, really. Ask questions, be honest if you don't have an answer, and engage your players to find a solution. It's okay, it's still your team, but now you have players willing to help shoulder a burden you've been carrying by yourself for way too long.

DEALING WITH CONFLICT

How do you deal with conflict or issues with your team? Have you attempted techniques that haven't worked previously? Are they totally against all you believe? Let's think for a moment about your perspective and what might upset you. What would you do if someone broke in front of you (in a *long* line) as you waited to buy your son or daughter a holiday gift last thing at night? Would you look in disbelief and stew about it? Would you step up and say something? How about a person being rough on their dog and yanking on its leash as you walk by?

Both are situations where you could quite possibly vocalize your disdain for a person's actions or words. But will you do that or justify it by thinking that's 'just my perception' and that 'it's only a gift, or it's not my pet'? Keep in mind these are incidents with total strangers, and we don't have any idea what their reaction is going to be (or maybe, more importantly, the whole story).

The person who jumped in front of you in line could be with someone holding their spot, and the pet owner may be using a technique you simply don't agree with, not necessarily abusing their pet. So, how does this relate to our team?

We ask team leaders – every day – to hold their teammates accountable, but at this point, we are asking too much. Have you trained them on how to approach teammates, allowed them to think what might upset them, what tone to use, to research the whole story, and not rush to judge the situation until they have all the facts? Let's remember that applies to us as coaches, as well.

As a team exercise, why not ask your players to write down three situations that would upset them if they saw it happening? Then, have them share these things with the team. Ask if they would step in or say something. What would make it easy to intervene? What would make it difficult? Could they do that with a teammate who's a friend? Then, explain how these actions are all about holding someone accountable.

Every conflict is different with your players. They vary depending on the situation, the player or players involved, how it impacts your team, and how you'll approach it.

The first step is to gather all the facts if you didn't witness a particular event. At this point, you must decide if it's an issue you need to be involved in, or whether you should let it go for now and see what happens. Another way to look at it is by asking yourself, "Can my team leaders handle this?" If not, after reviewing the facts and talking to all the players involved, you have a decision to make. Will you hold them accountable? What will make your decision easy? What will make it hard? I know – when it's a player who's done everything you've asked for four years – and now makes a mistake, quite out of character, it can become a tough situation to deal with.

I believe the trigger for that decision is your perception. And that stems from what upsets you, what you cannot live with within your team, and how you feel it may affect your team. In essence, you're in that checkout line and someone has cut in front of you. You know someone wasn't holding their spot. What will you do next? Simply looking on in disbelief and being upset will not help your team. Often, you must step up, be vocal, and hold players accountable.

I will mention one point here to keep in mind at the very beginning. Ask yourself, "Am I the problem?" Am I creating issues through favoritism towards certain players? Am I being too harsh on other players? Does it appear I don't care? By hoping this issue plays out, am I making it worse? They are all questions to consider as you move forward in the process of dealing with conflict. Just remember to look in the mirror and be honest with yourself.

Let's mention steps to consider as you move through accountability.

Rather than calling a player out, you may want to consider explaining what you see to the team. Be specific in saying this conflict must stop now, and that you respect their ability to make that happen. If that doesn't work, bring the individuals in, and talk about it.

Share what you know, what you've learned, and your responsibility in the conflict, if any. I might note here that even if you haven't contributed to any part of the conflict, it doesn't hurt to share what you think you *could have done* in some small way to prevent this.

Explain that conflict is not new; you've seen it many times, and it happens with differing views and opinions. Then, paint a picture of how you see this playing out if action is not taken, and why it's necessary. Remember, not everyone will be happy with the outcome.

Give the player or players time to explain their side of the story. Listen intently without interruption. When they finish, remind them they can move past this moment and show their teammates what they are made of. Emphasize your commitment to help them in any way possible.

Also, remember, off the field as well as on it, players are the first to know they've made a mistake. There's no need for long lectures or stories about what you've seen or experienced. At this point, it falls on deaf ears. Hand out the accountability, move on, and hope that – at some point in their life, when they're honest with themselves – they'll understand to some degree what they might have done differently.

As a coach, you have a team counting on you. You soon realize that by not stepping up and confronting conflict, you are creating a situation you can never recover from.

DECISIONS. ARE YOU CONSISTENT?

Decisions command our involvement, our attention, and – ultimately – our leadership in moments big and small throughout our careers. There's no avoiding them. Some are easy, while others require long consideration and thought. Many involve the game through strategy, lineups, and set pieces. Others are laid at our feet concerning player accountability when individuals do not live up to expectations. Did you give this much thought as you entered your coaching career? Without any experience, I'm guessing not.

We got into coaching because we had a passion for the game. We knew what it took to play at a high level, and we simply wanted to lead a team to greatness. Has that happened over your coaching career? If not, there can be many reasons, but have you ever considered how it might have something to do with your ability to deal with and make decisions? Especially the tough ones.

Fans and parents, for the most part, only see the game, the substitutions, and the plays. They have no idea of the day-to-day operations of your club or team and the variety of decisions you face.

Let's explore the result of not providing the leadership necessary to solve challenges with your team. Have you made a decision you later regretted? Not one involving the game, but one involving accountability, for example. How did it impact your team? It's a given (and a constant theme of this book) that if you don't hold a player accountable – because of their status or skill level – it will cost you more than any loss. It can be a tough lesson to learn and may have long-lasting consequences for your season, credibility with your players, and your career.

What questions do we usually ask ourselves or consider when a decision is laid on our desk?

1. Who's involved?
2. What exactly happened?
3. Did it break an expectation?

4. Where is the accountability here?

As you talk with the player or players, you'll be able to answer most questions, and the subsequent decision will be clear. Or will it? Here's the point. Some coaches make a bad decision worse as they think of the following five considerations when the accountability issue involves sitting a player out for the next game or games.

1. This player has never been in trouble throughout their career.
2. We have a big game tomorrow night, and I need them for the game.
3. Let's delay the punishment until we play a soft opponent.
4. Can I change the accountability to lessen the punishment?
5. What if they just apologize to the team?

What new standard are you setting by changing accountability? If this incident happened recently with a player who rarely plays, did you consider or allow them to go unpunished? I'm guessing the answer is no.

Before you enter the Pittsburgh Steelers locker room, there's a sign that simply says, "The Standard is the Standard." It says nothing about being the quarterback, wide receiver, leading rusher, or highest-paid player. Would that sign be appropriate to your leadership with respect to accountability? Only you can answer that.

How can some coaches be so strong in this area, while others toss and turn to decide? I believe it comes down to two things.

#1. Be consistent in every decision you make. When you are, your players will watch a teammate make a mistake and say, "Oh no, they are in trouble now. Coach won't allow that to happen."

#2. Always do what's best *for the team* by holding players accountable and following the expectations you and the team have built.

In essence, our decisions are based on consistency and integrity, regardless of who the player is, or what they bring to the team.

Remember, players expect to be held accountable, and when we do anything less, our credibility is eroded. Perhaps more importantly, we lose the chance to influence a player's life in a positive way by getting them back on track. Being a coach isn't a popularity contest. At the time, a player might not like being held accountable but, in the end, they'll understand they are part of something bigger than themselves.

A coach once told me, "Son, the decisions you make won't keep you awake. It's the ones you keep putting off, or try to get around, that will eat you up."

I believe it's in our coaching DNA to look ahead and attempt to see every turn in the road facing our team. Often, we are tempted to straighten the curves or take a detour when considering our schedule, a particular player, or our own beliefs. When we do, it's usually based on thoughts of, "They're a good kid. They didn't mean to do it. It really wasn't their fault. Those other kids started it."

I know you want to lead your team to greatness. There will be situations you hadn't planned on as your team watches your leadership, and records your decisions. It may cost you a win, a district or conference title, or a chance for a player to break a personal or team record. It's not easy holding a player responsible when the team needs them, but keep in mind their decision wasn't made by you, and by doing nothing, you stand to lose much more: your team.

Be that *consistent leader* who operates with *integrity*, allowing players to do what they do best: play the game. Greatness may or may not be on the cards, but you'll have a group of players who know they can count on you – as their leader – to do the best for them!

DOUBT. CAN YOU LET IT GO?

Coaches face a multitude of challenges every day. Some we know are coming, while others appear quickly and without warning – like a summer thunderstorm. Many are easily solved from experience, while others linger and are tough to deal with.

Here are a few worth mentioning:

1. Fired after the season
2. Confronted by an angry parent
3. Little support from administrators
4. Didn't sign that special player
5. Player(s) leaves the team
6. Players feuding with each other
7. Losing season
8. Best player lost for the season with injury
9. Your decision cost your team a game
10. Blasted on social media

I know you could tell me 10 joyous reasons that justify why you should continue to coach and make you feel great. But our focus is on the tougher side of coaching, and how it impacts you and your family's ability to cope and function.

If you coach, there are probably at least three memories that bother you to this day. They are impossible to forget; you still feel they were unfair, and you believe you could have handled them better or made different decisions.

Mental health and coaching are not often linked together in coaching education classes. Yes, they are vaguely mentioned when dealing with an angry parent, controlling yourself in confrontations with officials, and managing your demeanor with players, but what about our previous list of challenges? What about *coaching doubt*? It is not a phrase or concept widely discussed; indeed, it is mostly avoided.

Why do we shy away from this topic? I believe the first and most obvious reason is we feel it makes us look weak to our players, parents, and colleagues. It doesn't matter if we are men or women; as coaches, we like to deal from a position of strength/power. In essence, we like to project that we can handle anything!

As we explore the issue of why we might experience doubt, the causes range from seemingly minor issues to career-altering experiences…

- The season is over; what now?
- How did we lose that championship game? Will we ever be there again?
- Maybe it is my lack of ability, with so many people saying it's true.
- I just got fired; where will I go from here?

During the season, we find ourselves busy – every day – with tasks for our team. Then it's over, and we feel lost. If we were in a championship game, we tend to beat ourselves up if we lost, feeling we let our team down through our decisions and preparation. When we have several parents or fans questioning our ability to coach, it hurts, no matter how tough we appear to be. And if you've ever lost your job, that's probably one of the roughest days in your and your family's life.

During doubt, we're in a fog – unable to sleep, listless with no energy, and continually thinking of ways we could have done something better to change the outcome of a game, a moment, or a decision.

So, how can we work through these moments, which can range from a day or two to weeks?

To a small degree, we have the perfect prescription right in front of us… our players. Have you watched with wonder when your players are emotional and upset after a heartbreaking loss, and then they are magically okay the next day? It's called resilience. They always have an overabundance of it, and we seem to be running on empty.

There is one other reason. All their interests aren't contained solely within the game. In essence, they can show sorrow for a little while and then move on. For us, our livelihood is all about the game. Do you have friends or colleagues you can confide in, outside interests, or activities outside the game? Escaping, if only for a little while, is essential for our mental health. We won't be able to leave our thoughts behind completely, but for a few moments with our friends and family, we're able to put them away and enjoy those who mean so much to us.

Completely escaping an uncomfortable moment, a decision that didn't work out, or a confrontation with a parent is impossible. What we do afterwards determines whether the moment owns us, or we move on. Think of it this way: the game, your school, your players, and especially your family mean so much to you, and that's why it hurts. That doesn't mean you accept it or like it; it just means your idea of being strong means it won't ruin your career.

Remember how I said earlier that I know you could tell me 10 joyous reasons that justify why you should coach and which make you feel great. Write each one down right now on a piece of paper, fold it up, and put it in your billfold or a safe place. When things aren't going your way, pull the sheet of paper out and remind yourself why you coach. That sense of relief, satisfaction, and even a smile won't be far behind. Your players need you, and those who know you will always believe in you. Keep your reasons for coaching handy and visible when you need a reason to smile about your job.

If you need more affirmation, call that colleague who knows you better than you know yourself. They've been there. Smile; it's time to start working on next season's schedule and get on the recruiting trail.

FRAMING A SUCCESSFUL PROGRAM

Have you ever considered how building or framing your program is similar to building a house? I'm sure you've driven through a new subdivision and seen houses in various stages of completion with the framework exposed.

What makes up the bones of your program? What's the first thing involved in building a house? The foundation. For us – in building, framing, and shaping a team – the foundation is our coaching and leadership philosophy. It has to be strong and built on principles and values that hold up all we believe.

Here are four components of that foundation you may want to consider:

1. **Shared Expectations.** It can't just be *your* team; it has to be the players' team as well. Without taking ownership, they'll play the game without any meaning, emotion, or commitment. Include your players in deciding what those expectations are, and you'll see a team that is *all-in*.
2. **Motivation/Inspiration.** How will you motivate and inspire so many different personalities? Should it be your job? How will you make your program the one every player wants to be a part of?
3. **Moral Compass.** It's about ALWAYS doing the right thing, even if it's tough or it hurts. Your players will always be watching.
4. **Accountability.** If you make a mistake, admit it. If players make a mistake, they have to be held accountable. Never waiver in your responsibility. Respect will be lost if accountability is lessened due to a player's status on the team.

Staying with our 'building a house' analogy, we'll need vertical walls or studs to give our house shape, support the siding, and connect our roof. They have to be strong, or our walls and roof will collapse.

For us, those vertical walls would include Planning, Challenges, Education, Staff, and Support. Let's look at each one and hear why they are important.

Planning - Be diligent. Priorities, Practice, and Training Sessions, as well as Scheduling, are key parts of planning. Deciding on our needs for next season is critical. Develop a blueprint of what you need to accomplish and adjust it as needed. Be sure to include the team when talking about needs and deficiencies. They are the ones who take to the field and have a sense of what it will take to be successful.

Support - Be magnetic. Meet regularly with your Athletic Director, letting them know what you need. Be involved in school activities outside your sport. Students and faculty need to know who you are and what you stand for. Supporting other programs gives others a reason to support your team. Get out in the community, let leaders know what is coming up with respect to your team, and ask for their assistance. Never take for granted the fact that fans will show up for your games or fundraisers without an invitation. Be proactive.

Education. Acquiring Licenses, Levels, Diplomas, and engaging Mentors are the most utilized and recognized sources of education. Investing in our coaching education through local, state, and national organizations allows us to learn new and current techniques, strategies, conditioning, and leadership ideas, as well as broader trends and techniques.

Staff - Communicate. Do your best to utilize your assistants in a way that makes them feel needed and important. Give them specific duties and responsibilities and seek their opinions and perspectives in key situations, such as game strategy and personnel moves. Let them run practice whenever possible. When hiring assistants, look for coaches who may not always agree with you in every situation. If you both agree, one of you isn't necessary.

Challenges - Resolve. Challenges from players, parents, and decisions will always be a huge part of the coaching profession. How we conduct ourselves when talking with an upset parent or player will play a big role in resolving the issue or making it worse. Remember to listen to what they have to say before jumping in, and never feel like you have to win every battle.

As we all know, houses don't always look the same on the outside. Sidings vary with wood, vinyl, brick, or stone. Roofs are different colors and textures. They are both what people see as they drive by. What would our fans and others observe when they see us play? Here's our list:

Skill. Developing an individual plan with each player will help improve their game and allow them to be responsible for getting it done. Work with each player when deciding what's needed. If it's *their* plan, they are more motivated to work it. Repetition is the key. When practicing with the whole group, make every activity game-related with pressure. Your opponent isn't going to make it easy for you, so our practice shouldn't reflect that condition.

Strategy - Adapt. Who you start, who can play, game plans, and set plays all need to be addressed before game day. Make a list of all players and possible positions they could play if needed. Rank them as well. Game plans should be based on the scouting report from other teams as well as what you and your staff know will work. Most goals are scored on set plays; while it takes time in practice to set up these situations, make sure you practice at least one.

Chemistry - Build. Developing team chemistry can be tricky with some groups and may require patience. I believe you can promote it through encouragement, holding players accountable, and being honest and frank in all you say to your team. When they know you'll take care of the tough decisions, regardless of who the player is, it lets them concentrate on what they do best… playing the game. Teams are brought together not by your strong leadership but by your consistent leadership.

What about our roof? It needs joists to hold it in place regardless of the toughest and harshest weather conditions. What components of our program would support our roof and help us when we face challenges?

Players - Enable. Every season, you should evaluate your players even if you've had them for more than four years. They need to hear where you think they stand, what they can accomplish, and how the team is depending on them. We often talk about the mental side of the game, and I believe you can accomplish that better in the off-season in a classroom setting. It's another great way to utilize an assistant coach. Players also have to know their roles. Let them know what you see, and ask what *they* see.

Vision - Paint it. Every season may require painting a *new* vision of your program, based on last season's results. That vision should be crystal clear to your boosters, administrators, and players. With a vision comes the requirements to make it happen. Do your best to get everyone on board and excited for what is possible. Let your players know it won't necessarily be easy, but the rewards will be worth it.

There are so many facets and components of leadership you'll need to consider as you frame your program. While the ones mentioned above have served us well, it doesn't mean they're the best for your program. That's one of the joys of coaching: designing your own blueprint for that beautiful house you and your team will build and making it able to withstand the toughest of times.

The framework can be changed at any point to suit what you and your team need. It is, however, nice to come back to – year after year – as a starting point in putting together a team that is a shining example of what *you and your school stand for.*

HONESTY, DO YOU LIVE IT?

Coaching is all about how you respond and adjust. At least, that's what I was taught and heard as a young coach. It is worth mentioning that some individuals will try to influence you regarding lineups, eligibility, playing time, awards, making concessions, and even offering rewards. I can assure you these are not mentioned in most coach's training sessions or courses. So, my questions are, "What will you do?", "How will you respond?", "Who will you turn to?", "What adjustments, if any, will you make?"

My first sentence is about game adjustments and how to respond to pressure in a game, but that pressure will be at its *greatest* when faced with the topics I've mentioned and your internal struggle to deal with them.

Those topics aren't brought up by criminals or shady characters; they usually come from everyday people such as an old family friend, a parent, a player, a childhood classmate, a respected businessman or woman, a teacher, an administrator, or an influential booster or banker. In most cases, they have no idea of the position it puts you in with respect to your career and the team. So, how will you respond?

Let's explore one question which may help us find the answer. "Are you an honest coach?" What exactly does that mean? Most would say it's about doing the right thing, but others might say what if doing the right thing impacts the player or team in a negative way... should I do it and hurt the player? While some might think 'who will ever know', or 'everyone is doing it so it must be okay', what exactly does honesty mean to you? Would your players say you're an honest coach?

Honesty brings about many emotions as well as many responsibilities. Being honest is easier in situations when the answer is clear. However, the situation may pull you in a direction you shouldn't go when you know better. That may come from being obsessed with a big game, winning, championships, and personal achievements.

I know we'd all agree that when we aren't totally honest, we're the first to know, and it eats at us at night when we try to sleep, or during the day when we ask ourselves over and over, "Why did I do or say that?" When that happens, it creates hope where there is none. It's when we feel no remorse or don't believe we did anything wrong that we (and others who trust us) should be worried. At that point, we are buried in a blur of what is right and what is wrong.

Here are some questions and statements that, when presented, will give you the chance to speak the truth.

1. Will my child be a starter on the team?
2. Why isn't my child playing?
3. Can't you let him/her play even though they didn't pass that class?
4. All I did was miss the game bus. Why can't I play?
5. My monetary contributions are contingent on my son playing.
6. Make sure my daughter is on that all-tournament team; she's worked hard all year long.
7. (From the Principal) I'm getting a lot of pressure from Mr. Wilson. Make sure Bobby plays.
8. My family lives in another district. Can my son play at your school while we still live there?
9. Coach, why am I not in the starting lineup?
10. Coach, Sara has been acting out in my class. Can you help?

Many questions are simple and only require that you explain your expectations and hold the player accountable. But wait, if it was that easy, anyone could be the coach! Revisit some of our questions with the player involved being your best. Imagine it's the state or conference final. Now, would you be totally honest and do what's necessary?

Some coaches might bail out and make them sit the first game next season, but what if he or she is a senior? I've known coaches who ask the team to vote, knowing what that answer will be.

The questions we've mentioned all require an answer. Why not go ahead and be totally honest when first asked? Dancing around the answer in terms of "Well, if she works hard and improves, she has a great chance to start" – when you know it isn't true – only gives parents hope and will come back to haunt you. That's because all they heard was she was going to start. The same applies to playing time.

With respect to behavior in class and riding the game bus, those should be included in your expectations with regard to specific accountability. It is important to let teachers and parents know, so they aren't surprised or caught off guard.

Playing out of the district, or parents putting pressure on your Principal for their child to play, are out of your hands. Refer parents who live in another district to your Athletic Director; there is no need to get involved. While it might be tough, I'd let your Principal know where you stood with respect to playing time. For him or her to influence any decision you make is unprofessional, and I wouldn't let it go on for any length of time. Should it persist, I'd ask for a meeting with the Superintendent.

Being honest can be tough, but it won't keep you awake at night or make you beat yourself up with what you said. It certainly doesn't mean it's easy, but when you go in the other direction, it tarnishes your reputation and ability to positively impact those who count on you every day.

I would also say that honesty might not be taught in some players' homes, so be the example and teacher of values that will serve them well as they build a family of their own.

Go ahead, do the right thing and be honest. You'll feel better.

IMPACT

ASSISTANT COACHES, SEARCHING

Some of the biggest challenges head coaches face every year are evaluating their staff, retaining assistant coaches, seeing them leave for other schools or careers, or letting them go because they are unable to do their job.

It can be a Catch 22 when considering new assistant coaches because the good ones may not be with you that long. Why? Because their aspiration is to be a head coach. But should that be a reason not to consider someone who may bring everything you need to the team?

What about those who seem to be lifetime assistant coaches? The ones who have worked for ten or more teams (and seem to be at a new school every year) or those who have been with you for an extended period. Are they too comfortable and seem to offer less and less impact on the team as the years pass? On the positive side, they know the system and what you need and want, but is that enough? Do they have any fire and passion? Are they connecting with the players and helping them improve, or just showing up and going through the motions?

As the head coach, you have many responsibilities. When periods are spent constantly training new coaches, it takes valuable time away from your team.

Before we go on, let me ask:

What exactly are you looking for in an assistant coach? Why? Because I've found some coaches who just want a helper. Think about that for a moment. Could the assistants you've lost in the past have left because they feel they have more to offer and give and the knowledge they could contribute so much more? Areas might include:

- Game Management
- Game Strategy
- Practice Plans

- Substitutions
- Developing Leaders

So, where do you search for assistant coaches? School announcements, peers, club teams, parents, or colleagues whose opinions and suggestions you value might be an option. What about former players becoming part of the coaching setup? Is that a good idea or a last resort? Let's mention some reasons why former players might be a good idea.

- They know you and your system.
- The training regime is familiar.
- You know their work ethic.
- It could become their career.
- They are dependable.
- Keep in mind you will have to train them.

What reasons would keep you from hiring a former player as an assistant coach? Maybe their leadership skills and work ethic were less than stellar as a player. At this point, they may be too close to the players. Will they be able to work with former teammates differently as their coach? In essence, will players respect them? And with no training, you'll be spending a lot of time teaching them what you need.

In short, I believe the best situation to hire former players is when you have a veteran assistant coach who can shoulder some of the training with you as a mentor. Does your school have an assistant coach training class? Your Athletic Director could put it together with input from all the head coaches, and head coaches could also teach part of the class. It would pay big dividends, especially for teams and head coaches. That's the area where the most turnover occurs and where you need the most help.

What about parents? I believe this to be a tricky situation. The best parent with the best intentions will always have their child's best interests at heart. It can't be avoided. It could create a lot of animosity with players and other parents with the perception of favoritism, even if none existed. It also could put you in a precarious position if you decide not to play this coach's son or daughter. While this might happen with any player, now you have their parent beside you on the sideline. How will they react? How will it impact your professional relationship? These are all questions that should be answered in the interview process if a parent is to be considered.

One of the best resources for assistant coaches is retired coaches. Why? Because they still love the game, are always willing to give something back, aren't caught up in climbing the coaching ladder, and don't really need the money. They can be a calming influence on you and your players when needed and will have experienced just about every situation you will encounter on and off the field. Plus, their schedules are flexible and readily available in your area. You just have to find them!

My most important recommendation when hiring assistant coaches is to hire someone unlike yourself whenever possible. If you're fiery, hire someone who is calm. If you're calm, hire someone fiery. A clone that acts just like you and reads every situation the same does you no good. They bring nothing new to the table and are unable to give you a different perspective, whether it's a game situation or an accountability issue outside the game. You need every angle before deciding the right path, and that's what this assistant brings.

Assistant coaches can be a great resource and help lead your team to success when utilized correctly. It doesn't mean they will be highly visible during the game; their work is quietly analyzing situations without the pressure of being the head coach. If you were an assistant before you became a head coach, you know what I mean. It's an advantage every head coach must use. Ask assistants during the game or practice, "What do you see?" "What else can we do?" "Who can handle this situation right now for us?" and then let them talk. They see clearly without clutter or interference. And, ultimately, you may see it as well, but now it confirms your thoughts and allows you to make key decisions.

I would also add one critical point at this time with regard to earning the respect of assistants, as well as respecting what they bring to your team. Do your best to bring assistants together to ask for their input on a decision you are about to announce to the team. Whether it's a game decision or a decision outside the game, *seek their input first.* There may be nothing more to say, or they may just agree, but it shows you value who they are as valuable staff members.

As we move back to hiring assistant coaches, how can you improve your ability to hire the best possible assistant? If your concerns lie in technical or tactical knowledge, develop a list of interview questions for potential assistants. Go ahead and include game and accountability issues you've witnessed. Have them take the time to write down their answers. You will readily see if they have a different view (remember, that may be okay). Seeing it from a new perspective may give you pause to reflect and quietly think, "I never thought of it that way."

What more could you want from an assistant coach?

CHALLENGES WE CAN'T OVERLOOK

If you've coached for any period of time, you will have inevitably had to make some tough decisions about player conduct. Some are painfully obvious, while others seem to beg questions, such as "What was my player thinking?" "What was their intent?" "Did they really consider the consequences?"

While having clear expectations and accountability measures in place usually allows us to settle incidents expediently, dealing with negative player conduct is still a part of coaching that is not enjoyable (albeit necessary) for anyone.

So, what are some of the player challenges that will require your leadership? Think about your top five. Here are a few to consider as you choose yours.

- Disqualification during a game
- Missing practice
- Failing academically or disrupting class
- Blatantly not following instructions in a game
- Refusing to enter a game
- Influencing other teammates to disregard your instructions

As you think about *your* top five, and some of those mentioned above, it is obvious that some will fall under the category of *player accountability*, which you hopefully formulated with your players at the beginning of the year. These typically include missing practice, fighting, and disqualification. Drugs and alcohol are usually covered in your school's handbook.

It's those other challenges – such as refusing to enter a game, disregarding instructions, negatively influencing a teammate, or freezing a teammate out during a game – that require immediate attention, and which may or may not have been included in your expectations. That is not to say we need to jump to conclusions.

Time may be required to see who or what the real problem is. It may be more than one player, and the incident may not be what we think it is.

After experiencing these situations, a veteran coach usually sees things for what they are and knows (with almost certainty!) who is guilty.

Here are some steps you might want to consider:

- Avoid, if possible, confronting the player or players immediately in front of the team. Time allows you to gather your thoughts.
- Bring the player or players into your office the next day. Always include an assistant coach or Athletic Director in the meeting.
- Explain your view of the situation, and then be quiet. Let them respond.
- When they finish, assuming you were correct in your assessment, be adamant that you and the team cannot tolerate this behavior. At this point, you must decide if punishment is called for. If rules have been broken, never waiver. Hold them accountable.
- If punishment is warranted, make sure to let the parents know immediately.
- Never be swayed by an immediate apology. This defense mechanism may have worked many times for this player or players.
- Never consider the big game coming up or how the absence of this player will be felt when deciding. If you delay punishment until the big game is over, you'll lose any respect you had with your team.
- Let the player or players know that a second offense will involve the possibility of dismissal from the team.

Only *you* know the best avenue to handle a situation with your team. However, the choices will always be to look the other way, see matters with rose-colored glasses, or step up and hold your player or players accountable. When we don't hold them accountable, we set a standard of weak leadership and inability to make tough decisions. If this continues throughout the season, your team will end up in chaos.

For your words to have meaning throughout the season, your actions must say, "This is what our team stands for, and anything else will not be tolerated."

By doing so, you'll free your players up to do what they do best: play the game.

HOW WILL YOUR PLAYERS RESPOND?

As the season progresses, how will your players respond to adversity?

When the season began, hope, anticipation, and expectations were undoubtedly high as a coaching staff, and certainly in your players' minds. That first game with the uniform on is always one that every player looks forward to, but what about now, as the season begins to grind, injuries add up, tension mounts, and the competition becomes tougher? Will your players react differently? Are they ready for these moments? Is 'readiness' possible without experience in those situations? I believe it is, and we'll dig deeper a little later.

Let's look at situations that players may have to deal with.

Ridiculed by a teammate. When tensions run high in a game, players may confront each other for two reasons. 1. A teammate isn't doing their job, or 2. They want to push the blame onto another player by yelling at them.

A terrible game. Every player will have a bad game at some point in their career. It may go from bad to worse, courtesy of unnecessary words or actions.

Harassing opponent. One of the easiest ways to rattle an opponent is to get in their ear with trash talk. You can bet your team will face a player (or players) who tries every trick to distract them.

An injury. At some point, one of your players will get injured. Players who play through injuries are usually quicker to react negatively when bumped or shoved.

Bad loss. Having a tough schedule increases the possibility of getting blown out by a top opponent. Can your players keep their composure when the game is settled early with time still on the clock?

Never starting. There simply is no way every player can start. With 35 or more players, it's just impossible if your focus is continued success.

Mistake that costs the game. With all-out effort and determination comes the possibility of making a mistake that may cost your team the game. Should we be upset when our players did all they could, but we lost the game on a bad or careless decision?

Bad call by an official. Just like your players, officials can have an off night. Our players have to take care of what they can control, and officials are not one of those areas (like it or not).

Rarely playing. Some players may rarely make it into a game due to their ability and skill. Usually, these are players who contribute in other ways, such as exemplifying what a good teammate is, or how you can lead without playing.

Being questioned about a mistake. As a coach, you have to know what a player 'was thinking' when they made a mistake. And you do this by asking them. Let your players know that's your style, so they can be ready.

No effort from a teammate. If the game means anything at all to your players, then their expectations for each other will be high. Being and holding teammates accountable is a strong trait of championship teams.

Remember, the goal here isn't to have a team that lives happily every day, with everyone always getting along. I'm not sure that's possible with so many different personalities, viewpoints, and personal expectations built on assorted morals and values. Our responsibility is to teach players to respect other viewpoints and ideas while working through tough situations.

When searching for solutions to the above list of challenging scenarios, the first place to look is in the mirror. Are you adding fire to situations by yelling, screaming, and harassing officials, as well as opposing players and coaches? What's your demeanor on the sideline? At practice? Simply put, "Are players taking their cue from you?" We have to be a calming example and act like someone with the composure and steadiness that our players need.

I think we'd agree that we want fire in all of our players, allowing others to see their determination and effort through their words and actions. But are those words and actions helpful or a hindrance? Will becoming upset take our players out of the game mentally? As a coach, what can we do, and where can we turn? After reviewing our own examples, we need to look at our team expectations. Are they thorough enough, and have we consistently held players accountable when they lose control on or off the field? Were they built with our players' input? Have they bought into the culture we're building together and expect?

What about suggestions for working with, and preparing our players for, adversity?

In some situations, team leaders or coaches must be involved and prepared to make immediate changes. Other situations, however, may involve meeting with players on a regular basis to talk about the team, their progress and goals, and subjects that might be of concern. Players need to know they can come to you anytime if they are distraught or troubled.

The situations we talked about earlier are great examples to use in a leadership class to train players. I suggest role-playing every incident, with one person being the coach, someone else being the player or players, and another being a team leader. Set the stage with varying degrees of tension and come up with different solutions. Then, work towards an agreement. Moving forward, have your players also come up with situations that haven't been mentioned?

What specifically should we focus on as coaches?

Talk with them. Often and timely. Set up meetings every two weeks or sooner if you feel that works best for you and your players. If you sense something is wrong, use that intuition to set up an immediate meeting.

Be frank. Let players know where they stand and what is possible. Explain your position on playing time and starting, and if that isn't possible at this time, let them know.

One size doesn't fit all. Appreciate and recognize who players are, what motivates them, and what they bring to your team.

Understanding their differences will allow you to adjust your approach to best help them.

Control the controllables. Reiterate that your players focus on what they can control. Have them develop a list of what they can control and what they can't.

Tolerance. Players should seek to find answers from their teammates. Encourage them to find solutions and talk with each other concerning issues and differences.

Composure. Players should be the calming force in a storm when their team needs them. Ask them to explain how a player can have composure and still be fiery. Do we have someone like that on our team?

Set the example. As a coach, show your players what you want by your actions. Keep your emotions in check in tough situations. This doesn't mean you don't voice your opinion when needed; it just means you understand who's watching.

There are no easy approaches or perfect solutions to adverse moments in a game where emotions run high. Ideally, we don't want them to dictate the outcome of the game with unwarranted actions or words. Understanding our role and responsibilities as a coach, and preparing our players for those moments, will go a long way toward turning an adverse moment into an opportunity we can take advantage of.

Creating an awareness of how challenging situations impact the team, individual players, and a game's outcome, will cause players to reflect when they're upset or angry both during and following a game. Remind them that getting upset is normal, *it's what they do after* – through out-of-character actions – that could cost them more than they realize.

PEER PRESSURE, THE GREAT MOTIVATOR

Certainly, one of our biggest challenges as coaches is motivating individual players. I must admit I've tried many methods and techniques, just as you have. Experts talk to us continuously about intrinsic and extrinsic motivation, and I've certainly aspired to that approach, as well, with some success.

Hardline coaches of today (or in the past) profess that the only way to get the best from players is through discipline and being real. It can work, but it also creates a lot of fear and anxiety in many young players, often driving them away from the game.

Lightbulb moments have taken me back as a young soccer player, playing for a fire and brimstone coach, and later as a young candidate at Officer Candidate School in Quantico, Virginia, at the United States Marines Academy, driven by a relentless Gunnery Sergeant. In both cases, I was put in a position to lead my peers. I must emphasize there is nothing more daunting than leading those you've grown up with or are the same age as. As you know, peer pressure is intense. Those who excel can push aside doubts such as, "What if I make a mistake?", "Will they still like me?", "How will I handle issues?", and so much more. But as I looked back, I was always motivated by the group I was leading because I didn't want to let them down.

In both cases, as a leader of potential new marines in drills, fitness, breaking down a rifle, maneuvers, and formations, my objective was to put them in a position to succeed. In the Marines, as Candidates, we rotated as platoon leaders, certainly some with more experience than others. In sports, I was always motivated by the veterans. I simply didn't want to make any mistakes.

In both cases, my motivation was:

1. To not let any of them down by my actions, lack of effort, or determination.
2. To prove to myself and them that I was a capable leader and teammate.

When you think about it, it's easy to see that most of us are motivated by wanting to do our best in front of (or with) our peers. A packed venue or stadium of rowdy opposing fans can't compare to our thoughts of making a mistake with teammates watching and counting on us. We can escape the crowd when we leave the game. There's no escaping our teammates. It's a consideration every coach should factor in as they confirm their captains or leaders.

So, as coaches, how can we best utilize peer pressure in a positive yet challenging environment to motivate and educate our players?

One idea is to recognize and talk about peer pressure with your team in a classroom leadership setting. The first thing is to define what it actually means. "Sports peer pressure" means the influence exerted by teammates or other athletes on an individual to conform to certain behaviors, expectations, or norms within a sporting environment. Depending on the situation, they can be positive (like pushing each other to train harder) or negative (pressuring someone to take unnecessary risks to fit in). You may want to put this definition on the screen or on a dry erasable board for your players.

After you've had an open conversation about this with your players, put them in groups of three or four. The dynamics of each group are up to you, but it may be a good idea to mix veterans and new players, as well as highly skilled players with less skilled players. Their assignment is to come up with two examples of "Game Peer Pressure" and "Practice Peer Pressure" and discuss both within their group. They should aim to generate two examples of each.

Key questions for each group to answer might be:

Have you seen this happen? What was the outcome? Have you felt this kind of pressure? How did you deal with it? What can we do to solve it?

As your meeting continues, your players' examples will guide you and what you feel will help them through this challenge.

But what about practical activities for our players?

I can remember at the Marine Academy when we were put in groups of three in an orienteering competition over five miles. My job was to use the compass to navigate through thick mountainous woods and valleys to hit ten checkpoints on our way to the finish line. It was grueling and hot, the brush was thick, and if I was off a degree or two, we would lose time and the distance increased. The pressure was truly on me from the fellow Marines I had just met. We ended up winning as my teammates kept demanding the best from me and encouraging me.

So, what can we include in our practice to help build an environment of peer pressure and growth?

In preseason or once a week, when convenient, put players in groups of four or five with one less skilled or new player in early practice activities. Now we're forcing the less skilled player to improve and hoping the more skilled players will demand more and not tolerate mistakes. Peer pressure will be an obvious by-product of this setup. You will also identify potential leaders and their idiosyncratic styles for your team.

Situations you can manipulate:

- Place a player who lacks self-confidence among your top players.
- Place a less skilled player as the group leader where no one else can talk.
- Pair a new player with upperclassmen.
- Choose a less skilled player who is the only one who can score or defend.
- The group is penalized if they are last in a competition.
- Young players must complete a skill or task for the group's success.

After practice, seek input from your players. Was leadership present? How or who? Did their group experience success? What was it? Did they fail at any time? What was said or done at that point? Did you see an example of encouragement?

More questions can be developed. What could your group have done better? What are you most proud of in your group? Was there peer pressure? Did you experience it? Did it impact you or your group's success?

Mix up your groups every day, not just the players who need help the most. Progress the activities where groups compete against each other and the losing group is penalized. The fury that comes with losing is what you need to see because it puts more pressure on players to succeed. And that's what you'll need against those top teams in your conference and at tournament time.

Wanting to do your best for your teammates is the greatest motivator there is. As a coach, nothing else comes close to showing you if the game or teammates mean anything to a player. Find out today.

POSTSEASON, WILL YOU TRUST YOURSELF?

With the postseason right around the corner, where are your thoughts concerning your team? Is it hard to focus?

Postseason is a great time to showcase your team and all they've accomplished during the season, but are you a little apprehensive about what's happening next? It's expected to be so; there's no escaping the fact that anticipation brings a little anguish with it.

That being said, how can you best prepare, and what should you consider? Let's begin with a few questions. What's the soccer IQ of your team? What do they do well? What do you wish they could do better? Is there time to fix areas where they are lacking?

Looking at the above, is there *one thing* you can work on to improve any deficiency? I believe we often overload our players during practice in an attempt to solve every deficiency before the postseason gets underway. Are we asking too much of our players? Are we neglecting our strengths or taking them for granted?

Let's think about our first question, to which only you know the answer... what is your team's soccer IQ? How can you even measure it? From experience, I think it is based on years in the game, time with your team, and previous experiences of coaches and clubs. If yours is a veteran team, the IQ would naturally be higher than a very young team (most of the time). Why is that important? Because it figures highly in our ability to ask more of our players.

Soccer is a simple game full of complex and calculated decisions that are timing-based and skill-dependent. Based on that description, is there time to master four or five weak areas and new schemes in the week before the tournament? Or should you focus on one or two concerns, at most, that you can work on to keep things simple before the postseason begins?

I know from personal experience that I've attempted to work on too many situations during this time of the year, which can be confusing and frustrating for players. Plus, it neglects some of the great things we did during the season.

Another drawback is your players can sense the tension through your demeanor and everything you're trying to correct or create in a small window of time.

What would your players say the team needs to work on at this time of the year? Have you asked them? Again, you know them better than anyone else, and some teams have better leadership and stronger players with a higher soccer IQ. These players often understand what it takes to be successful in the postseason. But would it be a good idea to start today and seek their input?

Whatever your style, it will always come back to the fact that we are all fixers. We want to fix every situation, every mis-hit ball, every shot that goes wide, every save that is mishandled, every pass that isn't completed, every breakdown in our system of play, and every unsuccessful corner or free kick.

But we have to face the fact that, with limited time in the postseason, multiple fixes may not be possible. Having a 90-minute practice that involves 8-10 minutes on every deficiency your team has, will do little to correct the team's problems. It may make you feel better that you spent a few minutes on each thing, but was it quality time that will really help?

Think back to those games during the season when your team was at its best. What made them so successful? What did they do well? *Why* was that? Build on those strengths to carry you through the postseason. Being prepared is what you want. Simply changing or adding things to confuse the opposition may ultimately confuse your team even more. Put the game in your players' hands, based on what you've taught, and what they've learned and experienced throughout the year. Be at peace with the fact that your team has unique talents and abilities. Play to those in the postseason and never look back.

Should the postseason not go the way you wanted, make notes on what you'll do differently next season. If you weren't prepared, use this year as a building block to plan next year's practice schedule to cover particular aspects of the game. Every year is different, every team is different, and that's what makes this the best career you'll ever have.

OUTSIDE OR UNANNOUNCED LEADERS

Leadership challenges come in many shapes and sizes. Some are loud and obvious, while others may go unnoticed. Some may be from sources outside your team, quietly eroding your ability to lead effectively. So, what should you look for? Will you recognize these challenges before they become a major issue?

Have you had to deal with dissension in your team? What did it look like? Who was involved? How did you resolve it? There are a lot of factors involved that can promote or nurture dissension. Often, it's something that coaches set the stage for by inadvertently showing favoritism to a certain player, or by being inconsistent with our expectations (based on the player involved or the perception that playing time isn't based on skill and ability). Dissension may also stem from a player who is not one of your chosen leaders and who has influence over a certain group of your team. Behind the scenes, they can be doing their best to destroy any chemistry your leaders have established. Or it can be a parent who's coached some of your players and who is now contradicting what you're teaching because they feel they know your players better than you do.

One of the key opportunities for dissension is with a new coach, or when a large group of seniors graduate and selfish underclassmen hurry to fill any void with self-serving motivations.

In the case of a new coach, some players see it as a chance to establish their territory and dominance over others. They believe the reason they didn't play had more to do with the former coach than themselves. Ultimately, they're testing your strength to lead. The key here is your ability to read the signals and see the indicators. In my case, it was pretty obvious as we headed to team camp. It didn't take a genius to know that my biggest challenge would be to bring this team together. At camp, as I observed the players, I noticed they sat in three distinct groups. There were several upperclassmen who didn't want to recognize the more talented younger players, the players who just wanted to play and had no time for squabbling. How in the world would I bring them together? I'll come back to that in a moment.

What about parental interference? Not necessarily a parent telling their child to do the exact opposite of what you asked them to do in a game (although that needs to be addressed), I'm talking about a parent who seizes an opportunity to influence your team or a group of players. If they've coached some of your players in club ball, they may make game suggestions while the players are at their child's house. In their mind, they're just trying to help the team, but it may be – and usually is – contradicting something you're working to establish either strategically or mentally.

Let's revisit that new team. What does dissension look like? Cliques, selfishness, no discipline, and self-appointed, self-serving player leadership. Should we be concerned with how it got this way? I don't think so, especially if it's your first year with them. You could have a meeting and lay down the law or what you expect, and while you may feel it's necessary, it may not be the best approach early on.

This will be a watershed moment for your career. While your intuition may tell you to share everything you see wrong at this moment, I wouldn't recommend it. I believe it just fuels the flames and creates more distance between you and them. I would only talk about what they can expect from you, your philosophy, and a few challenges you've faced in your career with other teams. Let them know every player will have a chance to prove why they should play. Put their minds at ease. At this point, they are all uneasy with a new coach and want to protect what they had with the former coach, or prove them wrong. While we know that isn't possible, they need to be able to hang onto that hope. There's no instant solution. Establishing your credibility through perseverance and consistent decision-making will take time.

In my case, there wasn't a magic formula or secret potion. At one point in one particular season (early in my career), I was certain we wouldn't win a game. However, we ended up winning three. It was the worst season in my career with respect to winning, but in so many ways, the most rewarding. My growth as a coach was off the charts. How can we learn in a comfortable, cozy setting? Only through trials and tribulations do we grow and discover the best ways to guide our players.

What about parental interference? Can we control parents? No, but we can explain – at the very first meeting – that we need their support even in the toughest of times. Remind them there may be occasions when their son or daughter calls them wanting to quit the team. It's not new, and while you can't tell them how to be a parent, you can suggest they remind their son or daughter to talk with *you* before making any decision. Emphasize that quitting isn't the answer. Explain your philosophy and that your door is open if they need to discuss concerns.

How about that player who is undermining you and your team leaders' decisions behind the scenes? I believe you have two choices. One is to identify them and step in immediately. Bring them in and find out what's going on. I've found that most of the time, this person will deny it's them. Or have a team meeting to let the team know what's going on. Whoever is involved will be dealt with if it doesn't stop. While this seems like an easy solution, I've found it only resolves problems for a little while. You will have to deal with this player or players at some point, and that decision may mean letting them go from your team.

Keep in mind that some decisions aren't clear-cut or easy. Take the following, for instance. What if the player involved is your most skilled player? Your three best players? What if five players threaten to quit if you discipline their friend? What if the player is the son or daughter of a prominent business person or the Principal or President's son or daughter? What would you do?

Challenges like dissension and outside influence will always be there… lurking just under the surface. Your leadership and ability to select the best leaders with your team will underscore why working with and for each other is the best path. Will you be tested? Without a doubt! Whether you pass that test is up to you. Understand that dissension – at its source – is small but its influence can infect your entire team. Attack it with every ounce of energy and determination you have, removing the source if needed. Your team is counting on you.

WHY WON'T THEY BUY IN?

Have you ever noticed reluctance in a new player's eyes and body language as you addressed the team in that first meeting? We may think it's because they're unfamiliar with what it takes to play at a high level or haven't been asked to do more, but is that it? Let's back up for a moment.

Think about your current players. Did you go overboard at their signing? It seems every school does so, whether it's Middle School, High School, or College. Often, they celebrate new players with elaborate singings, the biggest and best in theatrics, giant screen video clips, and a fanfare with large crowds.

While all of that is nice, and we're elated for players who can play at the highest level, we're left to wonder how far it can go. After all, they've yet to play a game or show what they can do for their new team! When the celebrations are over, what will we see when it's time to go to work? Will they prove what they're capable of as a team member?

But let's get back to that look, that body language. Where does that originate? A lot comes from the disappointment that the celebration is over. Now they're in a meeting with no one holding them high, or they're doing fitness tests and battling veterans in small-sided games. Those moments when they felt they were the greatest player in the world – destined to be the game changer for your school and your team – are gone. How can you bring them out without destroying that vision of what they mean to the team?

This all leads back to our title and buy in. It's easy to buy in when they first get an offer to play as a high-profile signing, but it may get a little tougher, with doubt brewing, when they become #30 of a 35-player roster. Why should they buy in? Can they actually do it? What could we have done to prepare them better?

Personally, I feel it's more important today *than ever before* to establish connections with every player. While being realistic about their current status and potential to contribute, it's vital to highlight every attribute that drove you to sign them.

I recommend having a meeting with all signees individually before school starts. Aside from players being realistic about the nature of their potential contributions (as above), it's imperative to explain your philosophy and the effort, commitment, and determination you expect to see. By painting that vision and what you expect, players will be better prepared for that first day of practice.

Also, remind them how many players are on the team. Underscore that for them to contribute, they will need to demonstrate relentless effort to prove they have what it takes.

Here are six vital areas to build on to help your players buy in.

Build connections. Just ask questions and let them talk. Why do they play? What other talents do they have outside the game? Where have they traveled to? Do they have any pets? What are they majoring in? If they could have any career, what would it be? Where would they live if they could live anywhere? What upsets them the most? What will make them a special teammate? Use whatever questions you feel are appropriate. It's just a way to get them talking in a comfortable setting.

Engage and involve players. Find ways to engage players mentally and physically through challenging and highly competitive practice activities. Also, take the time to seek players' input on varying the activities and do your best to incorporate some in your practice. Consider including your players in establishing rules and expectations for the team. Nothing gets them to buy in quicker than sharing leadership of the team.

Recognize the value they bring to the team. A simple recognition for the reserves: "We practice against one of the top teams in the state every day with our nonstarters," or an unheralded player on your team (mentioning them by name) during a TV or newspaper interview may be the spark they need.

Be what you want to see. Your work ethic and commitment send an unmistakable message. Come to practice early and get everything ready. Have a high-quality practice; stay and work with players who want individual skill work.

Show genuine concern. Greet your players as they arrive at practice with a smile and cheery word. As they gather for instructions, take the opportunity to share how blessed you feel to be their coach. During practice, engage them with questions concerning their decisions using the Good, Better, Best method. Have them think back on a particular decision and define it as good, better, or best, and if it wasn't the best, what would have been.

Be fair and consistent in every decision. Accountability is one of the toughest tasks in coaching, but if you included the team when establishing expectations, they know what the penalties will be. Base every situation on those expectations, regardless of status on the team, or whether the next game is a big game or not. Players are watching. Do what's right for the right reason, even if it hurts. You'll never regret it.

As you think about your players and the history of players buying in, I feel certain most coaches will have had varying degrees of success. Some players are just naturally skeptical for various reasons. It may be their nature; they may not like your coaching style or personality or be partial to another coach. Honestly, I feel there are some players you may never win over totally, and that's okay. Just like skill levels, you may be only able to take them to a certain level of buying in. If they're still able to do what you need for the team, then live with it. Buying in isn't a cure-all for your team, but when your effort is sincere, it will make a difference, even with those who are reluctant.

WILL THEY LEAD?

Often, a player you see as having the greatest potential to lead shies away from that responsibility, leaving things to a less than favorable choice. Why is that? Can you convince them to change their mind? What will it cost your team if they won't consider a leadership role?

As you think about this challenge, you must ask: "What do I see in this player? Why would they make a good leader? Have I witnessed a glimpse of their leadership ability, and ultimately, could I be wrong?" Your experience with other team dynamics gives you great insight into leadership potential, and it would be a strong idea to compare a list of qualities and characteristics behind good and great leaders *against this player*. What would your list include? Would it be influenced by a preconceived vision of this team's dynamics and what they need?

Most coaches' leadership qualities will be similar, such as strong character, integrity, willingness to step forward, holds teammates and themselves accountable, great work ethic, strong faith, honesty, commitment, determination, resilience, positive attitude, and many more. How does your player stack up against this list? Keep in mind it's only important they have the key qualities that *you* are looking for.

But wait, we may be getting ahead of ourselves. It doesn't matter if a player has all our qualities if they don't want or feel the need to lead. So, where do we go from here? Give up and move on, or should we be more diligent and keep trying? You have nothing to lose at this point, so why not find out the real reason they won't lead? There are many reasons or perceived notions, and I'm sure you've heard most in your career. Meet with the player and listen to what may be holding them back.

As you think about those doubtful questions or statements your players have offered concerning leadership, here are a few worth mentioning:

1. It's my senior year, and I just want to relax and play the game without any added pressure.
2. There are players on our team who I don't get along with, and I don't think I could make a difference or influence them.
3. Last year, the captains were really harsh, selfish, and created dissension. They really made me hate that role.
4. I'm concerned it could negatively influence my game. If I have to worry about ten other players in a game, plus the others on the bench, how will I be able to focus on my job on game day?
5. I'm not really good at holding a teammate accountable when they step out of line or aren't giving complete effort in practice or a game.
6. My personality is that of a quiet person. I'm not a yeller and screamer.
7. What would I do if it was me having a bad game, or wasn't doing my job? I'm supposed to be the leader.
8. How can I be the leader, I don't even start. How could the team respect anything I say when I'm not in the game?
9. In my freshmen year, I was out of control on and off the field. While that has drastically improved, there are a lot of players on the team who remember that side of me. Why would they listen to me?
10. What will I do when another player becomes upset with what I've said or asked them to do? Who will help me?

All the above are tough questions or statements to answer. They represent legitimate concerns. Let's make this simple on ourselves and say you probably won't have to answer every question listed to convince your player to lead. But it doesn't mean you shouldn't be prepared for them at some point in your career.

Let's get to the underlying issue or concern you'll have to address:

1. **Doubt.** Any player who hasn't been an official leader or captain may have doubts about their ability. In the beginning, they're overwhelmed with a lot to think about

concerning the role. Remind them of the times you've seen them lead in an indirect way and been impressed. Build their confidence and let them know leaders take every situation individually and give it their full attention.

2. **Accountability.** Players have to think about holding themselves accountable first, and then their teammates. As a leader, it just means you expect the best from every player, knowing we all depend on each other. Remember, every player is different in terms of motivation and what upsets them.

3. **Past history.** Players who have been less than totally accountable may see this as a problem or something that will be held against them. The past is history. We all make mistakes and grow from them every day. Be that example for your teammates. If you owe someone an apology, take care of it; if not, move on.

4. **Friends.** One of the toughest parts of leading is understanding that you might have to hold your best friend accountable. Ultimately, it may cost you a friend. That's a price a potential leader must consider. As a leader, you're responsible to every player, and if your friend is out of line, you'll have to step up and take care of it.

5. **No training.** This is simple. A player just wants to know how to handle certain situations they've never dealt with. As a coach, it's our responsibility to provide that training for any potential leaders (usually in the off season). Get your class started as soon as possible, and watch your leaders grow.

6. **Demeanor.** Often, players have a vision of what a leader should look and act like from their experience. We know leaders come with different strengths and abilities. Some are vocal, while others are quiet. Some are confrontational, while others work behind the scenes. There is no set blueprint; it's just what works for the leader and is best for the team.

7. **Conflict.** There will be some conflict when you're the leader. The key is listening intently to both sides and coming up with a solution that both sides can agree on. It won't always happen, but as a leader, that's your

responsibility. There may be a time when you just have to say that's how it is, when one party doesn't agree. Just do your best to do what's right for the right reason.

8. **Pressure.** A potential leader may have a legitimate worry about pressure, and it may take away from their game. In that case, you must weigh how important their role on the field is, and whether they can do that and lead. Some can and some can't. If another leader can help shoulder the burden, that could be a possibility. Either way, you and the player will have to come up with what's best for them and the team.

9. **Status.** Young players may be more concerned with where they fit in – and the effort it took to get there – more than leading. The cost to lead is too high in their mind. Rarely can you overcome this objection. Your only reasoning has to be appealing to what they want to accomplish with the team. If that's not a priority, it won't work.

10. **Selfishness.** It's like one of our first statements, "It's my senior year, and I just want to relax, have fun, and enjoy the games without any added pressure." While we may not agree with their philosophy – and, honestly, this is one that really bothers me – they have openly told us they don't want to lead. In the long run, I think you'd agree you are better off without this player as one of your leaders.

There will be many challenges concerning leadership and your team. Finding the right player or players is only one. It takes a special individual to step forward and say, "Yes, I'll lead this team," and you may not know how special they are until you look around and no one else wants to lead.

It may take time for preferred players to assume any leadership role. Overcoming their objections, reassuring them that you will back them up in their decisions, and doing your best to train them may be all they need to hear. Some have said leaders are born, not made. I disagree. Those leaders that we feel were born into the role didn't have all the tools necessary to lead, but THEY WERE WILLING TO LEAD. That's the difference. Find those players on your team today.

24 TEAM BUILDING ACTIVITIES

SKI BOARDS

Each team is split into even groups on each end of a designated straight course. Groups of four players for each team must climb onto their pair of boards (skis).

One foot must be on each board while players hold on – each side – to a rope connected to the board. Then, they must walk the skis toward a finish line.

Players must travel past a cone, step off, and then turn the boards around. Waiting teammates must "drive the skis" back to the starting line.

The first team with all their players back is the winner. Players' feet must always be on both boards.

Google "Ski Boards" to see how easy it is to make your own set. You'll need to build two sets for the competition. You can also shorten boards for three riders instead of four. The task is easier for three riders.

PERSONALITY PUZZLE

Divide your team into groups of four. Give each group a small puzzle that should take about 20-25 minutes to complete. Before they begin, give each player one card with a "personality" (i.e., character) to assume and act out verbally while working on the puzzle and not give away the personality they are playing. Tell them to be as creative with their personality as possible.

At the end, go around and ask everyone to share what personality they were modeling. It's a great activity as players really get into their roles.

Here are some personalities you might want to consider.

CEO. You're assertive, data-driven, and born to lead. You value logic over emotion and freely express your opinions.

Charismatic. A social magnet who loves the spotlight and navigates social circles with ease. Your charm and creative expression make you unforgettable.

Critical Thinker. You prize logic and data more than emotions. Your love for planning and order rivals that of a chess grandmaster.

Free Spirit. You dance to the beat of your own drum, valuing emotion and creativity over cold, hard facts. You're the artist splashing colors on a canvas while others draw inside the lines.

Rational Optimist. Your interactions are uplifting. You naturally draw people toward you. You savor the present, enriching each moment with your greatest asset – trust.

Humble. You're the type who would rather direct the spotlight toward others than stand in it. In a world shouting "Look at me," you whisper, "How can I help?"

Introspector. You navigate life while others skim the surface. In a world addicted to the spotlight, you find sanctuary in introspection – where true self-discovery unfolds.

Nonconformist. You dance to the beat of your own drum. In a world that loves its boundaries, you're the one expanding them – and that's where the magic happens.

Passionate Dreamer. Your world isn't just black and white – it's painted in hues of emotion and daydreams. You're the one lighting fireworks of feeling.

Social Perfectionist. Your empathetic nature makes you highly sought-after. One who thrives in the spotlight helping others. Your presence draws people to you.

Social Butterfly. You effortlessly capture attention. You thrive in the spotlight, masterfully navigating the give-and-take of social exchanges.

Truth-seeker. When others nod and accept, you raise an eyebrow and manage challenges. You embrace complexities calmly, questioning existing paths and daring to carve out new ones.

Turbulent Spirit. You're a complex puzzle: a serene surface sometimes hiding turbulent rapids below. Your empathy shines through, but you also hold others to high standards and may grow frustrated if they fall short.

TIC TAC TOE

Two teams race each other to a Tic Tac Toe board and toss their markers (knotted pennies) onto said Tic Tac Toe board made with agility rings.

Each team is given three pennies of the same color. If there is no winner after the first three pennies are tossed, continue by switching each team's pennies already on the board until there's a winner.

Agility rings make nice playing boards. Beach balls make a good alternative to pennies. Make sure to tie a knot in the pennies for weight.

As a variation, have players go in pairs with one player blindfolded. The blindfolded player must place or change the penny.

REVERSE ORDER STEPPING STONES

Teams line up shoulder to shoulder while facing the other team. Agility rings are placed in front of each player, and players are asked to step into the rings.

The winning team is the first to reverse the order of their team's line-up completely. Players must move one at a time, left to right, and must not step out or fall out of the rings to touch the ground at any point.

HULA HOOP CHALLENGE

Players make a circle with arms locked together or holding hands. If you have a large group, you may want to split them into groups of eight or so. The coach or leader unlocks two players' arms or hands and places a Hula Hoop between them, before placing their hands or arms back together. The object of the game is to pass the Hula Hoop around the circle by stepping or passing through it until the Hula Hoop has traveled all the way around and back. If anyone separates their hands or arms, that team must start over.

As a variation, use two Hula Hoops per team, directly across from each other to begin with.

FLIP THE TARP

Begin this activity by having all team members stand on their tarpaulin (5 x 10 or 5 x 12 feet). Once everyone is on, they must work together to flip the tarp over – so they are standing on the underside – without stepping on the ground. The key point to make during this activity is that they can only touch the tarp, not the floor. The team must start again if any team member touches the floor.

Players are not allowed to get on each other's backs, shoulders, or jump in any manner. Fifteen to twenty participants is ideal, more than 20 and you should use two tarps.

TRUST YOUR TEAMMATE

This two-team competition uses small flat cones (or pie tins; they make a great noise if stepped on or bumped) as obstacles.

Mark off a long and narrow grid 30 x 10 feet, then divide the players into two or four teams. Allow the teams to divide themselves into pairs where one partner is blindfolded. That player will be walking down the grid blindfolded, from one end to the other, being directed by their partner and avoiding the obstacles. (Once over the other end, the participants switch roles and travel back.)

As mentioned, one player must guide their partner along the marked area to the other end without stepping on or bumping into any cones or pie tins. The player guiding their partner cannot enter the course and must walk along the opposite side of the course, while using verbal instructions to get their partner past the finish line.

Depending on the number of players you have, and how difficult you want this activity to be, you can vary the number of pairs trying to complete the course simultaneously, ensuring they work harder to listen to each other and communicate clearly. The winner is the first team to get all their players down and back.

If a participant steps on or bumps a pie tin, they must stop and count to five before continuing.

For variation, have groups of three on each team, with one group member directing both their teammates. In turn, have teams use numbers instead of regular commands (e.g., forward, backward, etc.) to direct their teammates.

10 LETTER WORDS TO LIVE BY RELAY

This is a two-team exercise where each team is given a 10-letter word. Use words that relate to your team, such as: confidence, commitment, dedication, determination, etc.

Write the words' letters on small cones enough times for both teams to each spell their unique word. If it's commitment (10 letters), you'll need 16 cones (total), which allows for the 10 letters to spell the words and six letters that are worthless in their grid.

Each team's letters are sprinkled in a designated marked square that is 10 x 10 or larger, facing each team at the other end of the gym or space. The decoy letters are mixed in to make the task more difficult.

Once the coach gives each team their word, they must run to collect the relevant cones, lining them up on the start line and spelling each word correctly. The quickest team wins.

ROPE KNOT GAME

Divide players into two or three teams. Have team members evenly spaced along a rope that has a single knot tied at each point where someone is standing, (seven members, seven knots, etc.). Each player must always have one hand on the rope (the same hand).

The object of the game is to untie the knots – sequentially – and have each team member step through the rope before the next person goes. The first team to untie their knots and have a straight rope wins.

ROPE CHALLENGE

Split your group into two teams. Use a large rope (½" to 1" thick; a tug-of-war rope works well), and have half the team sit down on one side of the rope and the other half on the other side facing each other. Everyone grabs hold of the rope with both hands, alternating hands with the person across from them. The challenge is for the whole team to stand up simultaneously while holding the rope with both hands. (Each team will balance the forces of the other as they try to haul themselves up.) Only one designated person is allowed to speak. Everyone's feet must begin flat on the ground or floor.

POSITIVE SIGNS

Here, you need marker pens, paper plates, and double-sided tape – preferably strong duct-like tape. (As a nice touch, you may want to design the plates resembling your sport's ball, e.g., soccer ball, basketball, etc.) Each player uses a piece of double-sided tape, sticks it on the back of their plate, and has someone stick the plate on their back. After everyone has a plate taped on, and a marker pen in their hands, the activity begins.

Walk around the area and write something positive or flattering/cool about that player on their plate. You can encourage them to write something positive about the sport they play, with respect to skill, etc. Make sure every player has a lot of superlatives on their plate before ending the activity. Afterward, you can have them tape their plate on their team locker to remind them what their teammates think of them.

FORM SHAPES/NUMBERS

Divide your group into two or three teams, with each team holding a medium-length rope. Each team's members should be evenly spaced along the rope, holding onto it.

Blindfold the team members and then yell out shapes (square, triangle, etc.) for each team to form. Progress up to octagons, hexagons, numbers, etc., and have a time limit.

A TEAMMATE'S VIEW

Cut pieces of construction paper of different colors into 1" by 9" strips. Have plenty of marker pens of different colors available, along with several rolls of scotch tape. Each player begins by writing their name and # on a strip of paper (they may decorate it also), then tapes it together to form a loop and passes it to the right to the person beside them. When you receive a player's loop, write something good or positive about them, decorate it, and add it to their chain by taping it together. Continue around the circle until everyone has a nice chain with lots of compliments.

CROSS THE RIVER

Use a 30-yard grid. Divide teams equally, then ensure that each team receives two towels. Everyone in each team stands on the first towel, and there will be an extra towel behind the last player. Members of that team must pick up that towel and hand it forward. Each player passes it up until it reaches the front of the group. When the front player gets it, they throw it out in front and jump on, followed by everyone else.

Players in the back continuously pass the extra towel forward, allowing the line to move forward. The winner is the first team to get all team members across the designated line. The object is for all team members to travel across the grid (river) without anyone falling off the towel. Towels can only go forward. The first team across wins. If anyone falls off, the team must start at the beginning.

As a variation, you can use rugs or small boards (rugs may get too slippery). Ensure that players hand their rugs or boards to the next player and don't throw them.

TEAM PUZZLE

Send your team picture to a website that creates jigsaw puzzles from pictures. Get the team together and tell them they're putting a puzzle together without letting them know it's a team picture. Bring popcorn and soft drinks to make it enjoyable. Make your players do the puzzle face down (i.e., viewing the blank side so they cannot see the picture on the front). This is a great analogy for not being able to see what the season will look like! You may want to have the website add a header or footer that says "CHAMPIONS" or you might want to hold back two or three jigsaw pieces as an example of what happens when all the pieces of a season – such as commitment, dedication, etc. – don't come together.

STAND ON A RUG

Divide your group into two or three teams. Use a 2 x 3' towel (small) or handkerchief. Players stand on the towel, and the object is for each team member to get at least one foot on the towel and one up in the air for at least 5 seconds. The first team to do so wins. Players are allowed to step on other players' feet that are on the towel.

CARRYING YOUR TEAMMATE

If you want a unique team-building activity, this is it.

Do an online search for army surplus stores and purchase two or four gurneys that are in good shape.

Set up an outdoor course where two teams can compete (make it more complex than a straight line… go under things, over things, etc.). Then, split the two teams into two sub-units – one at the start line and the other at the finish line. The object is for two carriers to carry a teammate to the other end using the gurney. Once each group has taken their turn as carriers, it's time to be the riders. Make certain players lay down completely on the gurney and are facing up in the direction they're being carried. Be certain to have spotters on each side of the gurney as it travels from one end to the other. Spotters should always be focused!

As a variation, it can be a good idea for another player (leader role) to walk with the gurney and instruct. They should encourage the carriers, especially when carrying a teammate for the first time.

If you have reservations about players carrying other players, find or buy two or three fence posts and have your players relay the posts in each gurney.

SCOOTER RELAYS

If you have time, and are so inclined, scooter relays are a competitive relay activity to try. You will have to purchase eight plastic elementary school scooters online and make some modifications. For older players, you'll need to bolt two scooters together to form one unit.

Two teams compete. Each active unit will consist of one rider and one pusher. When the starter command says go, riders and pushers will head to the other end of the course, where they will switch with two of their teammates. The team that gets all their teammates back to where they started will be the winner.

The rider should sit on the scooter and keep their arms and feet tucked in, so that neither are outside the scooter. The pusher will need to push the rider's back to move forward.

WATER CUP RELAY

Two, three, or four teams compete in this relay. Teams are in single file and lined up, side by side with their opponent. The first player in each line has a cup filled with water, while the other players have an empty cup.

When the leader says ready, the first person sits their cup of water on their head and holds it in place. When the leader says go, the second person holds their cup up close to the first person's cup to catch the water, and the first person pouring must tilt their cup backward so the next person in line can capture it. Continue down the line. After the last person gets his or her water, compare the final cup on each team to see who has the most. The team with the most water wins this activity. This team-building exercise is always fun to do at camp when it is hot.

POOL NOODLE PIPE RACE

This is a two-team competition. After the players are divided into teams, they select the number of pool noodles (pipes) equal to the number of players on their team.

Use a razor knife to cut the top half of the noodle off length-wise. Be creative in shaping them by making some short and some long.

The object of the game is to have a marble roll from start to finish, along each player's noodle, at least once.

Give each team five minutes to plan their strategy. They must line up shoulder-to-shoulder – holding their pipes waist-high and connecting the players' noodles beside them. This creates a track for a marble to travel along. Once the marble starts rolling, players must quickly relocate to the front of the line after the marble passes along their section of pipe, along the entire length of the team, before it lands in a bucket.

Players cannot cover one end of the pipe to keep the marble from falling. Both hands must be on the pipe. If the marble hits the floor, the team can continue by reloading the marble at that spot.

The first team to get their marble in the bucket is the winner.

Variations include moving the bucket farther away from the last player and having the line reform completely more than twice before any team can win.

AUTOGRAPHS

Make a list of statements (25) that players may have tried, visited, or accomplished. Print out the list, then give one to each player and have them interview their teammates. They have two minutes, and can complete the task individually or in small groups. Most autographs win. No yelling!

Find as many teammates as possible in two minutes who fit the characteristics listed below. When you locate a teammate, have them autograph your sheet.

1. Have won a championship_____

2. Have a birthday in DECEMBER_____

3. Have 6 or more immediate family members_____

4. Volunteers during the Holidays_____

5. Has a relative who played a sport in college (what sport)_____

Etc.

TISSUE RELAY

Line up in two or four single lines, side by side.

Pair up with a teammate, and ensure each pair has a beach ball and a tissue. Put the beach ball between the players, held in place by their shoulders, with the tissue sitting on top of the beach ball. When the leader says go, compete with another team to go around a cone and back without losing the tissue. Then, hand the tissue to the next pair on their team. The first team to have all players bring the tissue back wins. (If the tissue falls off, pick it up, reload it, and continue.)

TEAM SPELLING

Players work together in four-player teams to spell the word given as quickly as possible. The grouping is up to you. In the beginning, you might want to have a group of veterans or players who know each other to make the activity run smoothly.

Each group will be given a poster board, painter's tape (to hold the poster board onto a table or desk), large markers, and string or twine (enough for each player in a team to tie around their team's marker). Make sure the lengths of the string are the same. The marker is tied to the end of each player's string, so they each have a role in controlling it. Each player simultaneously holds the marker tight with their string in an upright position, allowing the group to move the marker and write a word – letter by letter – given by the coach. In the beginning, words should only be four letters, then progress to larger words, and finally, use words that relate to your game, e.g., dedication, commitment, etc.

For variation, mix veterans with rookies, or vary the length of the string.

HERO/HIGHLIGHT/HARDSHIP

This is a great icebreaker.

Have your players form a circle. When they feel comfortable enough, ask if one player will start the activity by sharing a hero, hardship, or highlight in their life. (Be patient, it may take a few minutes for a player to step forward and share.) Once done, encourage someone else to do it. This is usually a heartfelt activity with tears and emotions, but it is an inspiration to watch and listen to. If you use this, I highly recommend the coaches participate as well after all the players have gone. Make sure players know it's not required. I can assure you it will bring your team closer together.

Team Building Questions for Individual/Team Reflection.

As you bring your team together after the activities, it's good to get their feedback. Here are some questions to use. Alternatively, make up your own.

- What were some of the challenges you faced?
- What was your plan? How did you come up with it?
- Did you communicate well as a team?
- Did you listen to others?
- Did everyone have some input?
- What were the reactions when your team made a mistake?
- What is similar from this activity to your game?
- What is good leadership?
- Did someone take the lead?
- Can you have more than one team leader?
- Can you lead without being the captain of your team?
- What qualities does a leader need to be effective?
- Do you feel you worked well as a team?
- Did everyone agree on the best solution or plan?
- Did anyone on the team surprise you?
- Were you able to completely trust your teammates?
- Looking back, what do you feel is the most important element of teamwork?
- What question(s) would you add to this list?

If you want to see pics and or video clips of several of these team building games, visit our website. https://wisersportsleadership.com/image-gallery/

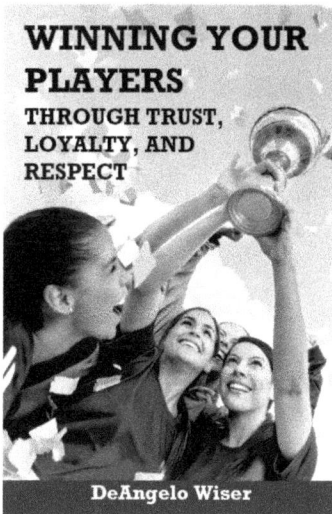

Winning Your Players through Trust, Loyalty, and Respect: A Soccer Coach's Guide

DeAngelo Wiser

In order to develop the best soccer players, who can achieve their very best in the game, a coach needs to instill three central qualities: Trust, Loyalty, and Respect. Without them, your words have no meaning and lack the power to inspire your players to reach new heights; with them, your team gains the ability and motivation to over-achieve.

Winning Your Players offers a clear pathway for coaches who want to develop and nurture talent to the best of their abilities, and gives insight into situations that require strong leadership at key moments with your team. In those moments we need every resource possible to clearly do what's best for our team. *Winning Your Players* is a must during those times.

Chapters include:
> Do You Trust Your Players?
> Eight Moments a Coach's Impact will never be Greater
> Can you handle the Truth?
> Over-coaching… can you hear it?
> …and many more

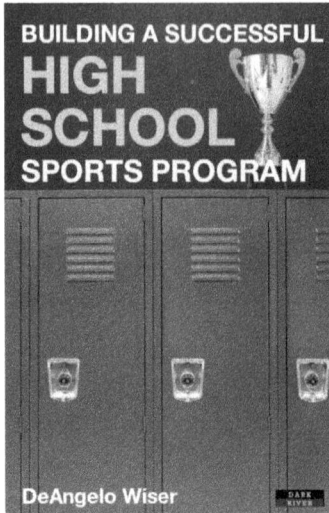

Building a Successful High School Sports Program

DeAngelo Wiser

Whatever sport you coach, building a successful sports program can be an enormous, sometimes daunting, task filled with many responsibilities and demands. Questions and decisions wait around every corner, often pulling a coach away from long-term considerations. How can you build a program when daily challenges require your attention?

In "Building a Successful High School Sports Program", former High School Soccer Coach DeAngelo Wiser addresses the fundamentals of building a successful High School program. He covers numerous topic areas including how to choose team players, bringing them together, managing expectations, how to define success, working with administrators and colleagues, tracking progress, dealing with personal adversity, and much more.

The book also includes contributions from a dozen highly successful High School coaches and Athletic Directors who offer decades of real-world wisdom and high-value advice. The book's foreword is by one of the world's leading and most recognizable Sport Psychologists – Bill Beswick.

Some of our other 30+ soccer coaching books

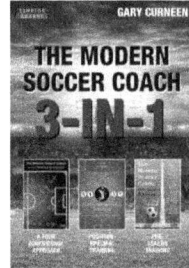

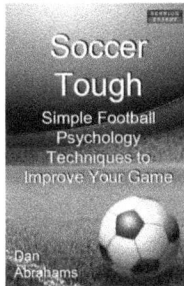

www.ingramcontent.com/pod-product-compliance
Lightning Source LLC
Chambersburg PA
CBHW050819090426
42737CB00021B/3437